W9-ACC-587

Stanley Weintraub is Evan Pugh Professor Emeritus of Arts and Humanities at Pennsylvania State University and the author of numerous histories and biographies, including *Silent Night* (available from Plume). He lives in Newark, Delaware.

GENERAL WASHINGTON'S CHRISTMAS FAREWELL

A MOUNT VERNON HOMECOMING, 1783

STANLEY WEINTRAUB

A PLUME BOOK

PLUME
Published by the Penguin Group
Penguin Group (USA) Inc., 375 Hudson Street,
New York, New York 10014, USA
Penguin Group (Canada), 10 Alcorn Avenue, Toronto,
Ontario M4V 3B2, Canada (a division of Pearson Penguin Canada Inc.)
Penguin Books Ltd., 80 Strand, London WC2R 0RL, England
Penguin Ireland, 25 St. Stephen's Green, Dublin 2,
Ireland (a division of Penguin Books Ltd.)
Penguin Group (Australia), 250 Camberwell Road, Camberwell, Victoria 3124,
Australia (a division of Pearson Australia Group Pty. Ltd.)
Penguin Books India Pvt. Ltd., 11 Community Centre, Panchsheel Park,
New Delhi - 110 017, India
Penguin Group (NZ), Cnr Airborne and Rosedale Roads, Albany,
Auckland 1310, New Zealand (a division of Pearson New Zealand Ltd.)
Penguin Books (South Africa) (Pty.) Ltd., 24 Sturdee Avenue,
Rosebank, Johannesburg 2196, South Africa

Penguin Books Ltd., Registered Offices: 80 Strand, London WC2R 0RL, England

Published by Plume, a member of Penguin Group (USA) Inc. This is an authorized
reprint of a hardcover edition published by Free Press. For information address Free
Press, A Division of Simon & Schuster, Inc., 1230 Avenue of the Americas, New York,
New York 10020.

First Plume Printing, November 2004
10 9 8 7 6 5 4 3 2 1

 REGISTERED TRADEMARK—MARCA REGISTRADA

The Library of Congress has catalogued the Free Press edition as follows:

Weintraub, Stanley
General Washington's Christmas farewell : a Mount Vernon homecoming. 1783 /
Stanley Weintraub.
p. cm.
ISBN 0-7432-4654-3 (hc.)
ISBN 0-452-28532-1 (pbk.)
Includes bibliographical references and index.
1. Washington, George, 1732–1799. 2. Generals—Retirement—United States—History—
18th century. 3. Farewells—United States—History—18th century. 4. Christmas—
Virginia—Mount Vernon—History—18th century. 5. Generals—United States—
Biography. 6. Presidents—United States—Biography. I. Title

E312.29.W45 2003
073.4'1'092—dc21
[B]   2003048343

Printed in the United States of America

FOR JIMMY AUSTIN AND NOAH AUSTIN
AND THEIR CLASSMATES AT
THE THOMAS JEFFERSON SCHOOL,
PULLMAN, WASHINGTON

CONTENTS

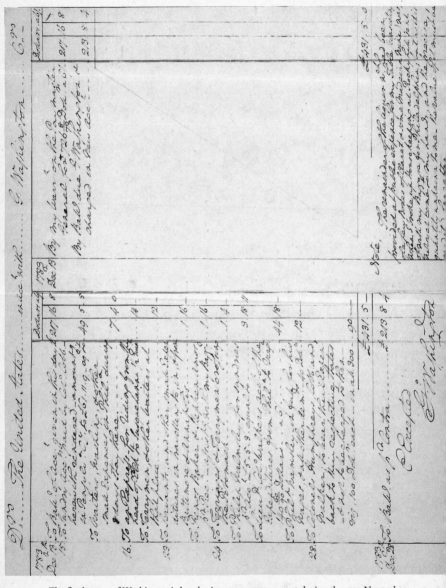

The final pages of Washington's handwritten expense account during the war, November —December 1783, showing his payments for entertainments, travel, servants, etc.

December

PREFACE

Not many Decembers ago, the teachers of my grandsons Noah and Jimmy invited me to talk to their classes about writing. The first and fifth grades at the Thomas Jefferson School in Pullman, Washington were not my usual audiences. I wondered what I might say that would be of interest to them. I hardly expected that what we discussed that wintry morning, as Christmas was approaching, would be of any importance. Still, a grandfather can hardly refuse such invitations. I even wore my "Grandad" T-shirt, given to me at Christmas the year before.

With two Founding Fathers' names in mind—their school and their state—I told the children about a book I was planning, set during the American War of Independence. They were excited to think that they were there at the book's beginnings. If all went well, the idea would materialize with chapters, and a cover, pages one could turn, and pictures. It would end, I explained, with the Revolution over and a peace treaty about to go into effect granting the thirteen American colonies their independence.

Some British troops remained in America in 1783, on orders to stay until ratification of the peace terms. Awaiting that word, George Washington longed to go home for Christmas. On the way to Virginia he intended to return his appointment as commander-in-chief of the army to the Congress in Annapolis, handing back the actual document he had received in 1775. Most regiments had already been disbanded; soldiers yearned to be back with their families before harsh winter weather arrived.

Late in November 1783, with Christmas only four weeks away, the General was still many miles from home. Before he could return to Mount Vernon, overlooking the Potomac River, he had one last mission to accomplish for the new nation. He had to reoccupy New York City, which the British forces were finally going to leave. Then the long war would really be over.

As I paused in each class, small hands shot up urgently. Some offered answers to questions I hadn't yet asked, even to questions I hadn't yet formulated. Did General Washington really get to Virginia in time for Christmas? How many miles did he have to travel? Did his army come with him? Was there fighting anywhere in America? What happened to the soldiers he left behind? Did he go home on horseback? Was there any other way? Did he have a favorite horse? What was its name? If there were no big bridges yet, how did Washington cross all the rivers? What rivers? (There must have been rivers.) What was Christmas like then? Did he have a Christmas tree waiting for him at home? Were Christmas trees that long ago like ours?

The first graders were half out of their seats. To many of them, Santa Claus was still real. They quickly brought him into the picture. Did Santa and his reindeer visit Mount Vernon, which must have had a lot of fireplaces? How did he know which chimney to come down? Were any little children there expecting Santa? Did Washington bring home any presents? How did he get them? Did children have toys then? Were they like our toys?

Some answers, many of which about that little-remembered month in our history were wrong, were shouted enthusiastically into other questions. There were more queries about what Christmas was like long ago. To some of the questions, I didn't yet know the answers myself. Still, their knowledge of our early history was surprising. Even the first graders knew about Paul Revere's ride, about Jefferson's role in drafting the Declaration of Independence (after all, their school was named for him), about the Liberty Bell, about Betsy Ross's flag of thirteen stars, and about many of the events that led to the victory at Yorktown, more than two years before Washington could finally start for home.

Before each class closed, each session seeming too short, I had learned how much those American beginnings still meant, even in distant states not yet so much as an idea in Washington's time.

I had also told the children about how all soldiers away at war at Christmas, since that day had become a family festival, especially longed for home. I recalled how I had spent two Christmases thousands of miles away during the Korean War, when many of their fathers and mothers had not yet been born. I did not tell them of the wrench to many soldiers when the Armed Forces Radio Network in Tokyo played "I'll Have a Blue Christmas Without You." The wry counterpoint to "White Christmas" would have been lost on them. Nor did I mention the sardonic GI responses to "I Saw Mommy Kissing Santa Claus," the irony of which appalled soldiers too far from home to play Santa themselves but worried about that somebody else behind the phony white beard.

"My war" seemed more remote to the children than Washington's, for it wasn't discussed in grade school, nor was Korea itself familiar on their broad roll-down classroom maps. Yet they knew about Washington and Jefferson, the Adamses, and Patrick Henry, even about such European volunteers as von Steuben and Lafayette, Pulaski, and the tongue-twisting Kosciuszko. Like many adults, they knew little about the two years of puzzling stalemate after the apparent finality of Yorktown or the ultimate withdrawal of the last British contingents from colonial America. But they wanted to know how Washington, and Christmas, fit into that story. I realized that I had a different book to write than I had first envisioned, about Christmas in 1783 and the memorable weeks in Washington's life leading up to it.

Few of us, children or adult, know of any traditional Christmas before Clement Clarke Moore's droll "A Visit from Saint Nicholas"—a generation after Washington—invented the sentimental American holiday. Our own Christmases are overwhelmed by a proliferation of Santas, electrically lit trees, and gift-wrapped packages and—even in rural eastern Washington—recorded carols blaring from small shops and through the corridors of glittering shopping malls. How different Christmas was in 1783!

Before that year, George Washington's most memorable peacetime Christmas was probably in 1758, although there was no Christmas in it. Excitingly to some, Halley's Comet reappeared that day to the unaided eye, as it did every seventy-six years, the last time before in the year William Penn landed on the banks of the Delaware. Very likely Washington never noticed it. He was twenty-six and it was his last Christmas as a bachelor. He spent the holiday—a dozen days before his marriage to Martha Dandridge Custis—riding about Mount Vernon to survey the expensive renovations intended to make his wealthy wife-to-be content. Plump, elegant, barely five feet tall, and the widowed mother of four small children, two of whom survived infancy, she was eight months older than Washington and had been the target of many suitors, as befitted the heiress of 17,438 acres of rich Virginia tobacco-growing land.

Washington's wartime Christmases would also have been difficult to forget. In 1776 he was preparing his troops to hazard the ice floes on the Delaware for a Christmas-night crossing to Trenton. In 1777 his depleted army, freezing and in some cases even shoeless, was trying to survive at Valley Forge, and he had ordered a squad from each brigade, with wagons, to forage among nearby farms to find the wherewithal for a decent dinner for his men. (He had reported grimly to the Continental Congress that his men had "not a single hoof of any kind to slaughter and not more than twenty-five barrels of flour.") That the calendar had again reached December 25 meant little, except to those whose enlistments expired in a week, with the new year.

December 1783 might have seemed to promise an era of peace on earth and goodwill toward men, at least in America, but the thirteen fledgling republics were flimsily united, without a compass to guide them into a nation. Many of the unsolved problems left by the long war remained. Returning to Mount Vernon, Washington could not escape them. His homeward journey would be an escalating triumph, a celebration of a human being as godlike as grateful Americans could envision. It would also be a test of his stubborn humility. Like the fabled General Lucius Quintius Cincinnatus of ancient Rome, to whom he would be compared, he hoped to withdraw from fame and return to his plough. But could he?

GENERAL
WASHINGTON'S
CHRISTMAS
FAREWELL

1

BEGINNING THE END

After more than eight years of war, General George Washington was impatient to return home. The unpretentious and unfinished country house, its wood panels shaped and covered with a sandy white paint to resemble stone, was still without a completed cupola and weather vane. Eight square wooden pillars already fronted the portico overlooking the broad waters of what was then known as the Potowmack. Mount Vernon and the postwar improvements he wanted to make to it had rarely been out of Washington's thoughts since the shooting had stopped. He had lived on the property, purchased by his father as Little Hunting Creek Plantation in 1735, since he was three years old. At nineteen, in 1751, he had inherited it from his half-brother Lawrence.

Since May 4, 1775, Washington had been back only once, for a few days in October 1781, during the culminating Yorktown campaign. Nearly fifty-two, his once reddish hair was graying above a Roman profile weather-beaten by early exposure as a surveyor, planter, and frontier soldier and etched by smallpox at nineteen. He felt physically and emotionally drained. In the limbo between war and peace, his weight, on a solid six-foot-four frame, had burgeoned to 209 pounds. To his worshipers, military and civilian, to whom he symbolized the new United States, Washington embodied rocklike persever-ance. He appeared even more majestic and larger than life late in 1783 than in his lean and anxious earlier years directing what seemed an unwinnable war.

Even then Washington had been a commanding figure. "You had prepared me to entertain a favorable opinion of him," Abi-gail Adams wrote to her husband early in the rebellion, "but I thought the one half was not told me." And she quoted to John Adams "those lines of Dryden,"

> Mark his Majestik fabrick! He's a temple
> Sacred by birth, and built by hands divine. . . .

Late in 1783 the letters of the Abbé Robin, a chaplain with Count de Rochambeau's army at Yorktown, had been pub-lished, with much the same view of Washington's "tall and no-ble stature," that "perhaps the exterior of no man was ever better calculated to gratify these expectations [of greatness]. . . ."

Since the shot heard 'round the world at Lexington had drawn him into the revolution, Washington had seen little of his plantation. Just before Yorktown, while preparing the siege of Lord Cornwallis's troops and hoping that the French forces he expected would not be outmaneuvered by a British fleet sailing from New York, he learned disquieting news. Fearing that British ships anchored in the Potomac below Mount Vernon were planning to burn the house, his distant cousin, Lund Washington, the resident manager of the home farm, went on board the enemy flagship to plead for the estate's safety. Assured that no harm would come to it, presumably as a result of a suitable ransom to which he agreed, he returned to Mount Vernon and arranged "as a present" to the British, he explained after the fact in a letter to the General, a consignment of sheep, hogs, and an abundant "supply of articles" including twenty slaves, flour from Washington's mill, and hams from his smokehouse. News of the shocking bribe also arrived through a courier from the Marquis de Lafayette, who was moving troops southward toward Yorktown.

It would have been "a less painful circumstance to me," Washington fumed to his cousin, "to have heard that in cause of your non-compliance with their request, they had burnt my house, and left my plantation in ruins. You should have behaved yourself as my representative, and reflected on the bad example of communicating with the Enemy." A "conflagration," he claimed, would have been better. Still, Mount Vernon had survived the embarrassing bargain, and—with Christmas approaching—Washington was now more anxious than ever to return.

On September 3, 1783, British negotiators in Paris had finally approved the treaty conceding American independence. News carried across the Atlantic by sail arrived frustratingly slowly. Nearly two months later, chafing in his dormant and depopulated headquarters, a two-story frame house at Rocky Hill, four miles from Princeton (formerly Princetown), New Jersey, Washington received confirmation that the "definitive" text of the treaty would be coming. The news was long expected, and long delayed, draining the event of any sense of elation. As early as March 25, word had come that the "preliminaries" to peace had been signed, but the back-and-forth of mutually acceptable language had to cross, and recross, both the Channel and an ocean.

In the interim, Sir Guy Carleton, British commander in New York and Long Island, the last major enclaves of enemy troops in the former colonies and home to resident and refugee royalists from Maine (then part of Massachusetts) to Georgia, had been slowly evacuating the area. The preliminary treaty articles had used the words "with all convenient speed" for the departures, but New York City and Long Island were being kept to guarantee an acceptable peace. Supplied from bases in Canada, the British also clung to seven isolated stockades on the American side of the Great Lakes, including Fort Niagara, Oswego, Presque Isle, Mackinaw, and the stockade at Detroit, intending to hold on to them until debts to be paid according to the treaty were duly settled. (The colonies were reluctant to make good, and it would be the mid-1790s before that happened.)

Fearing violence from returning patriots, some New York Tories had fled as early as April, mostly to Nova Scotia. While flotillas from England, Canada, and the Caribbean were assembling to evacuate further thousands of unhappy British soldiers and sympathizers, Congress began authorizing the discharge of Continental troops anxious to return home before the onset of winter. Delegates were eager to comply. The former colonies preferred having no standing army to paying for one.

Congress had overseen the war, and now the peace, almost without money and without the authority to coerce it from the states or its citizens. States retained sovereign powers; Congress under the Articles of Confederation, ratified seven months before Yorktown, was little more than a discussion group. Only South Carolina had paid its full 1782 quota to the federal treasury by July 1783 and had furnished that contribution "in kind" rather than in coin—supplies for the former army in the south, now disbanding at Charleston. Virginia had contributed half its quota; Rhode Island had paid a fourth, Pennsylvania a fifth, Connecticut and New Jersey each a seventh, Massachusetts an eighth, New York and Maryland a twentieth, New Hampshire less than 1 percent. North Carolina, Delaware, and Georgia had paid in nothing at all. Nevertheless, Washington would feel compelled to praise the states for their support of the war for their own independence. He could do little else.

From Newburgh, his New York headquarters on the Hudson during the early summer, he kept messages going to Virginia about readying Mount Vernon for its owner's return, deploring the loss of rents from defecting tenants and ordering supplies "for my Negroes." To his brother, John Augustine Washington, the General confided, "I wait here with much impatience, the arrival of the Definitive Treaty; this event will put a period not only to my Military Service, but also to my public life; as the remainder of my natural one shall be spent in that kind of ease and repose which a man enjoys that is free from the load of public cares, and subject to no other Controul than that of his own judgment, and a proper conduct for the walk of private Life." Yet he worried also about "the Affairs of this Continent" being "conducted by thirteen distinct Sovereignties." As commander in chief of the armed forces of the former colonies and their only unifying symbol, he wanted to see "competent powers for all *general* purposes" vested "in the Sovereignty of the United States" to prevent "Anarchy and Confusion." Effective with the peace treaty, he hoped that the nation, if it were one, would "set out right," for his "Army in the Field" could no longer unite the states. That army now hardly existed.

The only civilian balance to the Congress was the group of governors of the states, for whom Washington was often the only unifying contact. Few communicated with each other. At one point there had been serious talk of "the necessity of appointing General Washington sole dictator of America" to stop the drift into disintegration. Evading such gossip, the General drafted a circular letter to the governors maintaining that only in real union could America become a great and happy nation: "With our fate," he prophesied, "will the destiny of unborn Millions be involved." He had to keep both the disunited states and the discontented army together as they waited for the formal acknowledgment of definitive peace. Things could fall apart— even the treaty itself.

At West Point in mid-November, making his intentions to resign public, Washington had added to Congress's instructions for dismissal of most troops his own "Farewell Orders to the Armies of the United States," lauding his men for their endurance of hardship, even "hunger and nakedness." He urged each soldier to recollect "the uncommon scenes in which he has been called to Act no inglorious part, and the astonishing events of which he has been a witness, events which have seldom if ever before taken place on the stage of human action, nor can they probably happen again. For who has before seen a disciplined Army form'd at once from such raw materials?" Closing his "benediction" with the long-anticipated announcement that he was also about "to retire from the service," he wrote in the third person, "The Curtain of seperation will soon be drawn, and the military scene to him will be closed for ever." Rather than covertly promoting himself for some other role, he intended that to mean all public office. In England, when the letter was read, months later, at a crowded London coffeehouse, "every hearer," it was reported, "was full of the writer's praises; the composition was said to be equal to anything of antient or modern date." Washington seemed above human ambition.

His British counterpart Sir Guy Carleton had tried earlier to relinquish his own awkward command. The peace ministry in London had ordered Carleton to send part of his army (and possibly Sir Guy himself) to the West Indies, to defend the sugar islands against the French. Resisting what he thought was a no-win assignment likely to be personally costly, he claimed to be busy curbing corruption in the command he had inherited from Sir Henry Clinton, as well as negotiating with Washington for months on exchanging prisoners of war.

Carleton now had only about five hundred surviving Americans, while Washington, after Yorktown, held some twelve thousand British, German, and loyalist prisoners. Congress was demanding £200,000 from the British to defray their upkeep before releasing them. With the British government unwilling to accept Carleton's resignation (he was needed in New York to complete the evacuation), he had written to Washington that he was baffled by the Congress's stubbornness about release of the prisoners and could only assume that the Americans wanted "to bring the war to the last extremities of rage." His understanding was that warring nations, on signing peace agreements, exchanged prisoners, and he knew that his side had already returned naval captives from England although he had not freed any held in New York. "It has not been usual, I think, since the barbarous ages to use any menaces, however obscure, towards prisoners and still less to practice towards them any acts of barbarity. . . . There is an easy and honourable way for Congress to diminish the burthen which our prisoners occasion." That way was for them to "be now delivered up." Carleton had no idea how broke the Confederation Congress was, and why it sought a captivity fee. Money was desperately needed, but the delegates could not agree on how to raise it.

Sir Guy's prisoners of war, if officers, were billeted thriftily in private homes in Flatbush or consigned for security to the city's Provost Prison. The ranks were treated wretchedly, although occasionally permitted visitors (if they could manage the distances) who could bring them food and clothes. Encounters could not have been pleasant. Until March 1782 the British considered captured Americans as rebels rather than prisoners of war and confined them to rotting bottoms anchored off Wallabout Bay on the Brooklyn side of the harbor opposite Crown Point. Twenty such vessels had once been needed. The *Jersey*, a dismantled sixty-four-gun ship reduced to bare masts, had been known to inmates until its collapse into the mudflats in May 1783 as "hell afloat."

On other hulks in New York harbor, men without local relatives and friends lived in the clothes in which they were captured and suffered from typhus, dysentery, and scurvy. Often the worms in their rations were the most solid food they were served. Every morning all prisoners were aroused with the unchanged cry, "Rebels, turn out your dead!" There were always more dead. Thousands were buried in shallow pits at the water's edge, where the tides soon washed out their bones. Years later, on April 6, 1808, thirteen hogsheads (each the equivalent of sixty-three gallons) of remains, all that the tides had not taken, were interred in a vault adjacent to the Brooklyn Navy Yard. Almost as many soldiers had died in

British captivity (about seven thousand) as had been killed in action.*

On March 17, 1783, Carleton had learned that Sir Charles Grey was to succeed him, but only an announcement arrived, not Grey himself. A month later Sir Guy discovered that Grey would not be coming after all. Carleton was to continue with the thankless task of withdrawing the remaining forces in America, as well as all loyalists willing to leave. At the Charleston garrison, the lieutenant governor, Alexander Leslie, had been beset by pleas from South Carolina loyalists that they take their slaves with them. Carleton warned that only slaves boarded with written confirmation of their purchase, or who were legally to be set free, could be transported with their owners, as otherwise, as chattels, they could be considered stolen property. New York had not been thought of as a slave-holding colony, but its human property was only less visible than the southern variety. There were also about two thousand former slaves within the British lines who by General Clinton's proclamation had been promised their freedom from their former masters for loyalty to the royalist cause. Carleton could not relinquish them to servitude.

Shortages of shipping also delayed the departures. To bring the initial 39,000 troops to New York in July 1776, the largest military force ever landed anywhere by the British to that time, had taken 427 transports loaded with men and supplies, even with bales of forage for horses, and fifty-two accompanying warships. Reembarking the occupiers over many months had

---

*About 8,000 Americans were estimated to be have been killed in action—unit actions were small—and another 8,000 to have died of disease. Since only about 120,000 served under arms sometime during the war (of a population of about three million), the casualties were a substantial portion of the military force. About 10,000 British were killed; most of the 15,000 taken prisoner survived.

required at least as many sailings, as frantic sympathizers by the thousands (29,244 from New York to Nova Scotia alone), along with their goods, were also promised accommodation. Carleton's orders to departing loyalists were that if they were not ready to be mustered for boarding when their vessels were ready, they would be "precluded from passages at government's expense."

Rancor against the Americans, who had never attempted to retake New York by force, was an unforeseen obstacle. Just before Yorktown, Washington had contrived a deception on the New Jersey shore opposite Staten Island to make the British under Sir Henry Clinton wary of an assault on New York City, in an attempt to keep enemy forces from sailing southward to bolster Earl Cornwallis. Leaving only two thousand men, attempting to look like more, opposite New York, Washington had marched the rest of his dwindling army southward toward Virginia—the first time in seven years that he visited Mount Vernon.

The British had captured an American courier with thirteen letters, one from Washington to Lafayette, suggesting that the French fleet might not be able to arrive in time to assist in pinning Earl Cornwallis down in Virginia. Sir Henry Clinton's deputy, General James Robertson, assumed that New York City might be attacked while Washington delayed an expected assault at Yorktown. It could all have been clever Washingtonian disinformation. All that British troops in the city knew was that they had never been realistically besieged. Bitter at their uselessness beyond panoply and parades, they were leaving after years of firing hardly a shot in anger. A loyalist versifier, the Reverend Jonathan Odell, had even boasted in a couplet,

Back to his mountains Washington may trot:
He take this city[?]—yes, when ice is hot.

Sir Guy did not want patriot reprisals against his departing ships. Learning of incidents perpetrated by angry evacuees, soldier and civilian, who resented premature resettlement, he warned about the consequences. On October 27, as "General and Commander-in-Chief of all his Majesty's forces, within the Colonies lying on the Atlantic Ocean, from Nova-Scotia to West Florida, inclusive," he had issued, with Rear Admiral Robert Digby, who would embark with him, a proclamation warning violators,

> Having received information that an outrage has lately been committed upon an American vessel, in the harbour of this city, by seizing and destroying her colours, in a riotous and disorderly manner, which behaviour is not only a breach of the peace of the city, but has a mischievous tendency to prolong the animosities, which it is the design of the provisional articles [of peace] to assuage and extinguish.

> This is therefore to warn all persons whatever from offering any insult to the colours of any sovereign nation within this harbour, under penalty of being severely punished. . . .

Because a withdrawal was inevitably a time for breakdowns in discipline, Sir Guy combined, in his declaration, a pragmatic respect for orderliness and for goodwill. While acknowledging defeat, he also made it publicly clear to royalists that the supplanting authority, whether they liked it or not, was already a legal entity.

Demonstrating further good faith, Carleton apprehended New Yorkers who were counterfeiting and passing Robert

Morris's notes. One was a printer, formerly of Waterbury, Connecticut, ironically surnamed Poor, "taken with all his types," who had "counterfeit money of every kind, nearly two hogsheads; the greatest part were 15 dollars notes, poorly executed." Another was a former American army chaplain, William May, and three others were "refugees" from American territory, Sylvester Mason, Lemuel Nichols, and Dennis Flin. Sir Guy promised to send them into the custody of General Washington. Carleton also forbade royalist refugees from demolishing buildings in order to carry off "any stone, brick or frame" to future new habitations abroad.

While hinting to London for a peerage rewarding his complex and prolonged efforts, as he had only a mere knighthood, Carleton advised that a "wise and mild" government in Canada would contribute to keeping its newly arriving colonists loyal and could be a model for what he cynically expected would be a discontented future America. He suggested that the cabinet might want to prolong a settlement until the infant republic collapsed in intrastate dissension and Americans realized "the consequences of their own folly." But the successor to the failed wartime government of Lord North preferred to be permanently and speedily rid of the impossible Americans—impossible even to themselves, as Carleton realized.

The Articles of Confederation for the former colonies appeared unworkable. In 1783, only one man represented all the disunited states to their people—George Washington. The classics-educated elite in England had often bestowed Roman epithets on their former cousins, the enemy, and before the Cincinnatus tag gained currency, even the sympathetic Sir Horace Walpole had wryly referred to the commander in chief as "Caius Manlius Washingtonius Americanus, the dictator." Caius, tribune of the plebs, considered by the Roman ruling class a dangerous subversive, had led a band of freedmen and slaves. Washington, the modern Caius Manlius, was attempting the seemingly impossible feat of backing away from dictatorship while keeping the newly freed Americans together as a nation.

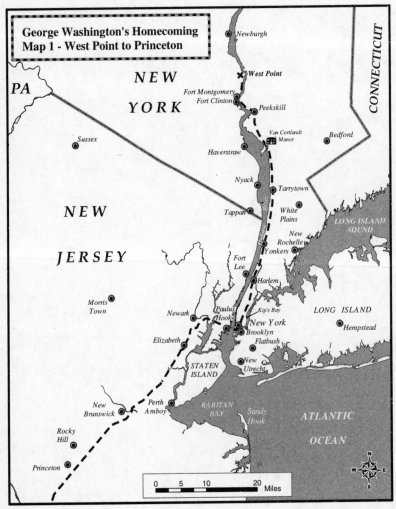

George Washington's Homecoming
Map 1 - West Point to Princeton

CONNECTICUT

Newburgh

NEW

YORK

PA

✕ *West Point*

Fort Montgomery
Fort Clinton
Peekskill

Sussex

Van Cortlandt Manor

Bedford

Haverstraw

Nyack

Tarrytown

NEW

Tappan

White Plains

JERSEY

New Rochelle
Yonkers

LONG ISLAND SOUND

Fort Lee

Harlem

Morris Town

Newark

Paulus Hook

Kip's Bay

LONG ISLAND

New York

Elizabeth

Brooklyn
Flatbush

Hempstead

STATEN ISLAND

New Utrecht

New Brunswick

Perth Amboy

RARITAN BAY

Sandy Hook

ATLANTIC

OCEAN

Rocky Hill

Princeton

0   5   10   20
Miles

N
W   E
S

Douglas Greenfield

November 17, 1783

2

THE PRICE OF INDEPENDENCE

Confirmation of final British departure from New York City and Long Island came to Washington in a message from Sir Guy received on November 17, 1783:

> The preparations for withdrawing his Majesties Troops from this place are so far advanced, that, unless some untoward accident should intervene I hope it may be accomplished some days before the end of the Month; in all events, I propose to relinquish Posts at King's Bridge and as far as McGowan's pass inclusive on this Island, on the 21st instant; to resign the possession of Herrick's and Hampstead with all to the Eastward on Long Island on the same day; to give up this City with Brooklyn, if possible on the day following; and Paulus Hook, Denyces [Ferry], and Staten Island, as soon after as may be practicable.

The harbor region and Long Island were a vast area to control with the few soldiers left to Washington, and he had even less of a navy. He would have to depend upon a reconstituted civil authority. In preparation for the reoccupation, he also wanted to make certain that as his troops entered New York, both its patriots and collaborators, long under cover, would be protected. Lieutenant Colonel Benjamin Tallmadge volunteered himself, he wrote later, "to insure the safety of several persons within the enemy's lines, who had served us faithfully and with intelligence during the war. As some of those were considered to be of the *Tory character,* who would be very obnoxious when the British army should depart, I suggested to Gen. Washington the propriety of my being permitted to go to New York, under the cover of a flag [of truce]." Conditions in the city were already sufficiently inflammatory that the British were eager to leave as soon as shipping became available. Once Tallmadge secured leave from Carleton, he trotted warily to the city, "where I was surrounded by British troops, Tories, cowboys, and traitors." ("Cowboys," originally a rural English term for unruly young men, were royalist rustlers and marauders once active on horse and foot as guerillas from Croton to Yonkers.*)

Received "with great respect," even by Sir Guy, "at whose table I dined with commanding officers of the navy, and others of high distinction," Tallmadge found it "not a little amusing, to see how men, Tories and refugees, who a little before uttered nothing but . . . *rebels and traitors to their King,* against all the officers of the American army, would now come around me . . . and beg my protection against the dreaded rage of their countrymen. But I knew them too well to make any promises." He

---

*"DeLancey's Cowboys," a lawless five hundred man corps from Westchester, had now retreated to Throgg's Neck on Long Island Sound. Known as "the Refugees," they were commanded by Lieutenant Colonel James DeLancey, son of Oliver DeLancey, a loyalist general. Their reputation was odious.

arranged for the safety of "all who had been friendly to us through the war, and especially our emissaries, so that"—he exaggerated mildly—"not one instance occurred of any abuse, after we took possession of the city."

Mutual hostility was inevitable. Incidents would be blamed on both sides. After dark one evening, Ephraim Smith, the royalist inspector of markets, "assisted by a party of soldiers," according to the patriot press, "determined that the DAMNED REBELS, as that *worthy character* is pleased to term them, should not enjoy so small a convenience when the insolence of his office shall be no more, cut down and carried to his house the bell of the Fly Market, with threats of prostrating the whole of the erections there." Sir Guy, "having been made acquainted with the transaction by a gentleman who happened accidentally to be present, . . . not only severely reprimanded Mr. Smith for his conduct; but Mr. Smith, by his orders, will have the mortification of replacing the bell in its old station." Another incident, less easily remedied, would occur with a flagpole, and still another at a newspaper office. Unfriendly feelings sometimes also arose wherever an excess of beer was quaffed or the defeated took umbrage at displays of the thirteen stripes.

The new flag was now ubiquitous, and in London a cheeky cartoonist in the *Rambler's Magazine* portrayed "Mrs. General Washington Bestowing thirteen Stripes on Britannia"—not the matronly Martha Washington thrashing Britannia, but Washington himself. Outraged, Britannia complains, "Is it thus my children beat me?" but the General, in drag, responds, "Parents should not behave like Tyrants to their Children." It pained the British to see the Washington who defeated the Empire as a woman in a three-cornered hat, suggesting in effect an amateurish militia besting an imperial army.

While troops waiting only to be disbanded were "impatient

to return to their respective homes," those "destined . . . to take possession of the city" had the satisfaction of a final mission. The fractious Congress seemed uninterested in any remnants of the army. It had been in session nearby at Princeton, where it had fled after the last mutiny of soldiers in Philadelphia, in January. In Princeton, which delegates detested as a miserable backwater, Congress had adjourned on November 4, intending to reconvene at Annapolis, Maryland, on November 26. From Princeton, "that obscure village," James Madison had reported unhappily to Washington, "Mr. Jones and my self are in one room scarcely ten feet square and in one bed." Joseph Jones was a large fellow congressman from Virginia. Charles Thomson, the Secretary of Congress, hoped that the change of venue, to a place known for its "balls, plays & assemblies," would reverse the monumental indifference of many delegates to legislative business.

En route home for Christmas, Washington intended to return his commission as commander in chief from what had been, in 1775, the Continental Congress. Like a practiced actor making his final exit, he wanted to achieve a dramatic public gesture confirming that a workable society that did not depend upon generals existed in America. He enjoyed the stage and often applied its lessons and employed its metaphors. "Nothing now remains," he wrote, "but for the actors of this mighty scene to preserve a perfect, unvarying constancy of character through the very last act, to close the drama with applause, and to retire from the military theater with the same approbation of angels and men which have crowned all their former virtuous actions."

Washington had aspired to high command in 1775, realizing that no other American was as qualified from authentic if not distinguished military experience. Conceding that shortage of expertise, Congress had jumped him four ranks from former British colonel (in the French and Indian War) to full general. Although, eight years later, there still seemed to be no one else to fill his tall boots, a civil society required a civil government. Early in the war John Adams had told another aspirant, Horatio Gates, English-born and once an officer in the British army, "We don't choose to trust you generals with too much power for too long a time." Yet Washington had seemed irreplaceable.

There was no way that he could justify his retirement before reoccupying New York, and that could not be accomplished before the British embarked. Other than to accommodate his desire to be back at Mount Vernon for Christmas, Washington had no need to hurry his departure. Given the difficulties of travel in American distances, and petty quarrels among the former colonies that augured poorly for unity (a few delegations were certain to stay away), the Congress could not expect to seat a quorum of nine states' representatives before December 13, if at all. The Maryland delegation might not assemble even in its own state.

To meet his personal schedule, Washington had, then, only a few weeks to wind up his official affairs and pass on the military succession for what little it would be worth. After Martha had visited him at Newburgh (where she had fallen ill with a fever) and returned with him to Princeton, he had sent her home to Virginia in early October—"before the weather and roads shou'd get bad," he explained in a letter to the Marquis de Lafayette. (Some later historians would invent her accompanying him home, even to depicting happy New Yorkers holding up their children to see her, and others imagined her returning from Mount Vernon to Annapolis to observe his formal retirement.) From Rocky Hill, the General had already ordered six transport teams under Captain Bazaleel Howe to "take charge of the Waggons which contain my baggage, and with the [armed] escort proceed with them to Virginia, and deliver the baggage at my house ten miles below Alexandria. As you know they contain all my Papers, which are of immense value to me, I am sure it is unnecessary to request your particular attention to them. . . . The bundle which contains my accounts you will be carefull of, and deliver them at the financier's Office [in Philadelphia, en route] with the Letters addressed to him, that is Mr. [Robert] Morris."

Washington would not risk shipping his precious papers by sea and had ordered "Six strong hair Trunks" (covered with hide retaining the hair) "well clasped and with good Locks," each with a brass or copper label with his name and identifying year. The route that Howe was to take would closely parallel his own, "through Philadelphia and Wilmington, thence by Elk Head [Elkton] to the lower Ferry on the Susquehanna, and thence through Baltimore, Bladensburgh, George Town, and Alexandria to Mount Vernon." They were not to make any water crossing "if the Wind should be high."

One group of papers remained to be organized and sent. On November 17, Washington had instructed Lieutenant Colonel Richard Varick, his recording secretary since May 1781 and in civilian life a lawyer, to "forward" all documents since October 1 to New York "before the first of Decr next." Everything else had been packed up for transport by Captain Howe. In Poughkeepsie, Varick and three clerks were busy transcribing and filing everything for Congress and the General, but a bundle of papers for October 1 through October 23 had not turned up. The next day Varick reported that the missing records had been "found in a Swamp, but that the Letters were too wet" to be copied or shipped. Apparently they had fallen off a wagon. Varick would send them to New York once he could rehabilitate them.

Washington intended to say his farewells, in person, to colleagues who had steadfastly remained in uniform, even when unpaid, and to revisit places that were already cherished locales of the conflict. He also wanted to establish continuity for the shrinking armed forces beyond his departure. The army was in danger of disappearing altogether as enlistments expired, units were disbanded, and funds to keep a national military entity functioning became more difficult to raise. Only with his final goals accomplished could he bid a formal good-bye to the difficult and often dysfunctional Congress, before which he planned to confirm his withdrawal into civilian obscurity.

On his first appointment in 1775, Washington had refused a then-substantial $500 a month for his services. He had never drawn a salary as commanding general and had asked for none, only for reimbursement of his expenses, which were substantial, given his aristocratic lifestyle. Much of that had not yet been paid by Congress. It had been difficult enough to get them to raise funds to fight the war. As late as January 1781, the year of the climactic victory at Yorktown and the surrender of General Cornwallis, the Pennsylvania line had mutinied for lack of payment of salaries, refusing suddenly proffered paper money that was worthless for anything but use in a privy. Several such incidents would embarrass the victors, including a more recent protest march in Philadelphia. The colonies had rebelled against paying taxes to an absentee king and were reluctant to assess their own citizens even in their own cause. The patriotism of Americans seemed to rise and fall on the price of independence.

From West Point on November 18, Washington had sent a courier to appeal to Robert Morris in Philadelphia for funds to pay his remaining officers. First came the good news, "the near approach of the evacuation of New York." The General enclosed a "Copy of a Letter from Sir Guy Carleton [which] will give you all the information I am possessed of on the subject." Then he wrote, "Knowing, as I do, the embarrassed state of our Finances, I should not at this time have troubled you with the representation of the Officers now in service, had not a Sense of their extreme distress overcome every other consideration." He assured Morris that with the departure of the last British garrison he would reduce his forces "very considerably, which will lessen the public expenditures in the same proportion."

As Superintendent of Finance, the portly Morris administered the chronically insolvent federal treasury, and he set about collecting "Notes and Cash" with little hope he could raise much. He would do his best, he replied to Washington, "but alas: Sir, the good Will, is all which I have in my power. . . . I am constantly involved in Scenes of Distress . . . and there is not any Money in the Treasury." "Cash" meant specie—silver and gold a soldier could try with his teeth—of a variety of origins: doubloons and dollars, crowns and francs, pistoles and thalers. Literally hard currency was a reassurance of enduring value. As Morris had confided to his diary on November 17 about the frustrations of raising money, "Haym Salomon says there is no demand for bills of Exchange, very few selling and the price falling." Salomon, a Polish-born Jewish commission merchant in Philadelphia in his early forties, was a principal, if informal, financier of the revolution and as Morris's broker acted without salary and even lent his own money with little expectation of repayment. Imprisoned in New York by the British as a traitor, he had escaped in 1778. Harsh conditions while a captive left him in poor health, and backing government loans would leave him impoverished.

Most troops had been mustered out during the summer months, but disbanding them peaceably (some had merely walked away) had required tendering some sort of acceptable money as separation pay rather than mere promises. They could not be safely returned to civil life, Morris had no need to warn Washington, "with murmurs and complaints in their mouths." That would create the conditions for anarchy or rebellion. To Theodorick Bland, a Virginia congressman, Washington warned that it was "an *indispensable* measure" that soldiers' accounts be settled before they returned "like a Sett of Beggars" to their states, and to Morris he estimated that three months' pay for each soldier would require at least three-quarters of a million dollars, a vast sum then, given the buying power of a single specie dollar, but even more immense when no hard currency was to be had.

All Morris could do was to print more potentially worthless paper, and he wrote to Congress that it was a matter "of great delicacy" to guarantee the redemption of notes to back the currency. "I hope, my dear Sir," he wrote to Washington, "that the state of public affairs will soon permit you to lay down the cares of your painful office. I should . . . have been liberated from mine if a desire to free you from your embarrassments and procure some little relief to your army had not induced a continuance of them."

On June 7, 1783, an earlier batch of Congressional notes had arrived from the printer, and in six days, at the risk of writer's cramp, Morris, burdened as well with his other duties at his cluttered finance desk, signed six thousand of them. The issue, at a face value of more than a million dollars, was made payable six months after the date on the face. Although the troops to be discharged would skeptically label the notes "shin-plasters," they had been distributed and quickly put into circulation. They were about to come due.

Now, Washington needed still more funds. Few soldiers

could afford to feed their families, and his harassed Quarter-master-General, Timothy Pickering, could seldom feed or clothe encamped men adequately. Among the economies ordered by Washington late in November was the shutting down of the Continental Hospital in Philadelphia, the last military facility, provided that the grand, high-walled Pennsylvania Hospital, the first public general hospital in North America, would accept (so Morris wrote to its reluctant managers on Washington's behalf) "these poor and unfortunate Soldiers who have lost their Health in the Service of their Country." Some had lost limbs as well as health, although crude amputation without disinfectants and anesthesia usually led only to agony followed by the grave. Morris guaranteed punctual payment for military patients "every three Months whilst I continue in Office" and warned the hospital officials of adverse "Public Opinion" if the terms put the Congress "to a heavy Expence."

Washington's active generals recognized the financial pressures on him from every direction, presenting him as he prepared to leave West Point for New York City, and home, with a consoling address. "If your attempts to ensure to the armies the just, the promised rewards of their long, severe and dangerous services, have failed of success," they wrote, "we believe it has arisen from causes not in your Excellency's power to controul." Without identifying directly those they and Washington understood were responsible, they rejected any idea that "the ultimate ingratitude of the people" would "shake the patriotism of those [soldiers] who suffer by it. . . . Most gladly would we cast a veil over every act which sullies the reputation of our country." They lamented the opposition to "those salutary measures . . . which alone can fix on a permanent basis the credit of the States," which seemed "essential to the justice, the honor and interest of the nation." The weakness of the union, they conceded, appealed to "the arts of false and selfish popularity, addressed to the feelings of avarice," and sullied the "reputation" and the "dignity" of the "respectable majority of the States."

Relieved at last from the "long suspense" of awaiting the treaty of peace, his senior officers also wanted to go home. "Our warmest wish is to return to the bosom of our country, to resume the character of citizens; and it will be our desire to become useful ones."

Washington himself intended to leave an inventory of his final official expenditures (even six pounds, ten shillings "to Barber at sundry times") and hope for the best. To him, "official" seemed to cover everything. Yet, despite huge losses in income during the war and much land left unproductive in his absence, he remained a wealthy Virginia planter and property lessor, although he could seldom collect, then, on his rents. He could afford, from his private purse, the best in personal uniforms and mounts and to maintain on his return his comfortable prewar manner, but he was also a proud man, and the new nation, inheriting a monarchical past, understood class privilege. His services to the new nation had left a hole in his comfortable life nearly nine years deep. He wanted at least minimal reimbursement and recorded—often estimated—his expenses liberally, even to charging interest on the use of his own funds. Washington would conclude on his return that he was ten thousand colonial pounds the poorer by his long absence, which might be reckoned (in purchasing power) as over a million present dollars. Yet he intended to "refuse," he told an aide, "anything that should carry with it the appearance of reward."

His oft-stated intentions to resign, now about to be realized, were so widely known that he continued to receive plaudits from England for forswearing ambition. The year before, the brief, troubled peacemaking ministry of the Marquis of Rockingham had given in to demands led by Irish politician Henry Grattan for legislative independence, whereupon the Irish parliament in gratitude had voted Grattan a gift of £50,000. Seven years before, his compatriot Henry Flood, a nationalist, had nevertheless accepted lucrative public office under the English. Both were now seen as opposites to Washington's seeming selflessness, and a London dispatch declared that the General's imminent retirement "etern[al]izes his character. From this moment he is to descend to posterity as the greatest man of the age in which he [has] lived. How wretched and insignificant do a Grattan and a Flood look, when set in comparison with him! The one receiving a boon of £50,000 for not serving his country—and the other holding back from the great object till the hazard was past." In this view from his adversary's side Washington "laboured for no emolument. He retires with no pension. Having begun and accomplished the deliverance of his country, having created an empire, he desired no other reward from the people that he had made free and imperial, than that they would love peace, do justice, and remember the debts which they owe to those who made them free." Yet the writer wondered whether unsophisticated provincials would indeed be reminded of their duty by Washington's noble "magnanimity."

3

TO NEW YORK CITY

On November 18, a Tuesday, Lieutenant Governor Pierre van Cortlandt left for Peekskill with Governor Clinton and his aides, crossing by ferry where the turbulent Hudson was still narrow, then heading southward on horseback. They stopped at the family manor at the Croton River overnight (the van Cortlandts had been a wealthy merchant family in New York since 1638), then slept on Wednesday night in Tarrytown, above White Plains, at the home of Edward Covenhoven. There they met Washington and his staff, who had followed the same route. On November 20 the group lodged overnight at Yonkers with Mrs. Frederick van Cortlandt. On Friday morning November 21 the cavalcade proceeded toward Harlem, to rendezvous with General Knox's encamped troops. Their progress, often within sight of the east bank of the Hudson, its rushing waters slate gray under late autumn clouds, was slow, but on schedule.

Whatever Washington's urgency, his timetable was at the mercy of the elements, unexpected emergencies, and the nature of travel. Horses, carriages, barges, sails, rutted roads (when there were any), waves, winds, tides, rain, and snow made even short journeys unpredictable and long journeys much more uncertain. There also remained the chance that along the way an unreconciled royalist might direct a musket ball at the man credited with separating the new nation from the Crown. To many of the king's fleeing subjects, however, Washington was less the victor of a war for independence than the benefactor of political radicals at home, who had undermined support for suppressing the rebellion. "Can Washington be called the conqueror of America? By no means," charged colonial New York Supreme Court Justice Thomas Jones from exile in England. "America was conquered in the British Parliament. Washington *never* could have conquered it. British Generals *never* did their duty. The friends of the rebel chief say he has virtues. I suppose he has; [but] I say, 'Curse on his virtues! They've undone his country.'"

From a Manhattan wharf to a Potomac jetty just above Mount Vernon was nearly three hundred miles by routes Washington would have to take. Although everywhere along the way he had promises to keep, the primary one was to spend Christmas with Martha. Since he wed Martha Dandridge Custis in January 1759, he had been absent on various missions, and then away for the war, nearly half their marriage. As he traveled south through New York City and Philadelphia he hoped to purchase further Yuletide gifts for her.

Many civilian diehards in New York City and Long Island had already embarked disconsolately for Jamaica or Nova Scotia, those sailing north promised 600 very likely untillable acres. Army officers resettling there were entitled to 1500 acres, and privates fifty. As a further and perhaps empty inducement, a settlement at the deepest point on Chedabucto Bay, well northeast of Halifax, would be named Guysborough, for

Carleton. (It still exists.) It was a rather empty gesture for an empty land, as disillusioned royalists arriving in the northlands reported that Nova Scotia had "nine months winter and only three months warm weather."

For England-bound passengers there loomed Atlantic storms and the near certainty of being at sea, if fortunate in remaining afloat, during the Christmas season. Their own reception would be disappointingly muted, as their support, however meager, continued the costs of the lost war. Only in 1787 did a novel appear exploiting their plight, *The Adventures of Jonathan Corncob: Loyal American Refugee.*

As early as November 18, Hessian mercenaries boarded troop transports for Bremen and Hamburg, "to the very great embarrassment," a patriot New York paper declared, "of their numerous creditors." Handicapped by a shortage of volunteers as the American war elicited little enthusiasm, the British government had hired 29,867 German soldiers from the dukedoms of Brunswick, Hesse-Cassel, and Hesse-Hanau, with a commission of thirty thalers (a little more than £7) per man to their rulers. Each *Landgrave* would also receive half more per wound and an additional third more if the recruit was maimed. Although the British needed their numbers, they despised the rough Hessians, who were never punished for plundering. The anonymous writer of *Jonathan Corncob,* who seems to have had wartime experience, would observe, "Whenever the troops of that nation saw any thing in an American house which suited them, they begged for it in a civil way; though at the same time using an argument that was unanswerable: 'If you vas one frynd to the Koning' said Lieut. *Hastendudenrot* of the *Trumbrick* regiment, 'you vas gif me your vatch; if you vas one repell, by Got I take it.'"

At least 5,000 mercenaries had deserted, 7,754 had died,

and many of the 17,313 who survived had been wounded or captured. Little more than half would return home. Before embarking his very last contingents from New York, Carleton had also sent convoys of 32,224 civilian royalists (and their property) to Nova Scotia, 1,328 to Quebec, and 1,458 to the Bahamas—a huge migration. Other than the remaining loyalist volunteers and the last of the mercenaries, he retained in his command only 1,930 British regulars.

Strategically useless to the British and expensive to maintain, the New York area had never been seriously threatened after its occupation. The Royal Navy had dominated its waters but required constant overseas replenishment. Washington had won without taking New York City by keeping enough of his small army intact over eight years to diminish any further support in Parliament or among the people for continuing the expensive and unwinnable war.

Even more depleted in numbers, Washington faced the prospect of leaving New York to the authority of Governor George Clinton. The army had no funds to pay troops to reoccupy the area, first seized by General William Howe in 1776. A staunch believer in the dominance of the states over any central government, Clinton was far from unhappy about this. Federal soldiers in the city would be largely a façade. Former residents, mostly believers in Clinton's views of state power, had been arriving for months to reoccupy their homes or to buy up loyalist property at bargain prices.

Washington's men had been marching in from West Point, their numbers small and symbolic, with Major General Henry Knox (to be Washington's successor) at their head. A onetime Boston bookseller who had become a master artilleryman (even his voice boomed), Knox at thirty-three seemed an army unto himself, his nearly three hundred pounds straining at the buttons on his Massachusetts uniform. He had first learned tactics, military engineering, and gunnery from his own books and joined a militia group, the Boston Grenadier Corps (less imposing than its name). In a duck-hunting accident in 1773, he blew off the two smallest fingers of his left hand but, despite the embarrassing handicap, earned his lieutenancy. On public occasions afterward he hid the hand in a handkerchief. Artfully, Gilbert Stuart, when later painting a half-length portrait of Knox, persuaded him to place his maimed hand on the barrel of a cannon in a way that concealed the missing fingers. (Virginian Richard Henry Lee, who lost the fingers of his left hand in a similar accident, wrapped the stump in a black silk handkerchief, dramatically gesturing with it as he spoke in the Congress.)

Several of Washington's generals exploited privileges of rank (as their commander sometimes did, with Martha) to have their wives with them, and even children, and a Newburgh farmer had petitioned headquarters to ask that several horses "belonging to Gennel Nox and family" be removed from his premises as they, and the family billeted there, were eating him out of house and home. Washington's entourage was indeed impressive in bulk and required vast provisions, forcing him early in 1783 to order families off army encampments. (Their horses, which each ingested a ton of hay or oats a month, remained.)

Several generals had stepped on the scales at West Point on August 19, 1783, during Washington's previous visit, and Benjamin Lincoln's weight was recorded by Washington's aide Lieutenant Colonel David Cobb (a puny 186) as 224 pounds and Henry Knox's at 280. Colonel Michael Jackson weighed in at a hefty 252 and Colonel, briefly General, Henry Jackson was a mere 230. Fortunately for the commissary, General Jedidiah

Huntington was a wispy 132 and General John Greaton only 166. At a time when average avoirdupois was far lower than today, only the wealthy—or those on expense accounts—could afford to be obese. Knox applied to the congressional secretary at war for an extra subsistence allowance while at West Point, to which the commander in chief added a friendly supporting letter.

To collect sufficient troops, Washington had left Princeton with his escorts for a final journey to West Point once his baggage train had departed. At Fort Lee, the western terminus of King's Ferry, he was delayed by an early snowstorm that blanketed the valley of the Hudson—still the North River to many. For nearly three days Washington remained near Tappan Town in the splendid but drafty mansion with whitewashed walls and high ceiling beams as the guest of Johannes DeWint's son-in-law, Fredericus Blauvelt. The wind off the river was strong and the fireplaces outlined with blue Delft tiles depicting religious scenes burned the year round, filling the house with smoke when the occupants closed all the doors and windows tightly to keep out "the foul night air."

It was the General's third use of the DeWint residence, and the only unanticipated one. There, in September 1780, Washington had brought Major John André for questioning after learning of Benedict Arnold's treason. It was one of the 280 houses in which he had slept during the war, Martha joining him at about ten of them, including the Rocky Hill headquarters from which she had departed to await Christmas at Mount Vernon. (He charged Martha's extravagantly costly visits to his expense accounts as "consequent of my self denial," explaining that it had been "to the no small detriment of my private Interest . . . to postpone the visit every year contemplated to make [to] my Family between the close of one Campaign and the opening of Another.") When the General moved in, the occupants had to move out, but Fredericus Blauvelt (the nearby town is now named for him) had other houses on his two hundred acres.

The Dutch Colonial brick DeWint house, built in 1700 from ship's ballast loaded in Zeeland, had been used briefly as Continental headquarters in 1780 and again for a crucial meeting with Carleton on May 4, 1783. Now, in the snow, Washington was greeted at the doorway by an awestruck Blauvelt child with an apple for him. He offered to share it with her, and with his pocket knife the General courteously divided it.

The postwar conference had prepared the way for the evacuation of New York. But for signatures the revolution was long over, and Sir Guy had sailed up the Hudson to Tappan under a flag of truce to initiate discussions about final withdrawal. It was the first time a representative of Great Britain had accorded the new United States the honors of a sovereign power. Lieutenant Colonel Richard Varick, then assisting General Philip Schuyler on Washington's behalf, recalled that the British "were received and saluted at Tappan by Maj. [Hamilton] Fish's detachment with drums beating and colours flying and afterwards by . . . the 2nd New York Light Infantry."

Following the formalities, Carleton's entourage, including Hessians who referred to General "Wassinton," retired to the south room with the Americans "to open the business. . . ." The tall, oak-beamed "Good Room" was too spacious to heat properly in winter, when the river often froze from shore to shore, but its ambience suggested authority. "About three hours after," Varick wrote, "a most Sumptuous Dinner was prepared . . . & about 30 of us sat down and ate and drank in Peace and good fellowship. . . ." (The charges, lumped together with other conference costs rather than listed separately, were noted by a newspaper in Philadelphia as exceeding £500.) Among other decisions, the parties agreed that "the carrying away of [unregistered] negroes"—slaves—"or other American property" would be impermissible, and that American "commissioners" could be on site "to inspect all embarkations." Over three thousand slaves would depart the city with their owners in 1783. A few were reclaimed by Washington's commissioners for lack of documents. Most sick, aged and helpless blacks, judged worthless as labor, were cynically abandoned by the British.

To complete arrangements the next morning, Washington visited Carleton's ship, HMS *Perseverance,* an occasion marked by the firing of a courteous seventeen-gun salute from the vessel's twenty-four pounders, after which, according to Varick, an "Elegant Dinner (tho not equal to the American) was prepared and we sat down in perfect harmony." With Carleton had been his closest associate in New York, the loyalist lawyer, Judge William Smith, who tried to extract some optimism from the circumstances. "I could not find Reason," he wrote in his diary, to discredit the Suspicion that Washington may be of the Party in Congress with the American Agents in Europe to bring about a Reunion." When he realized unhappily that Sir Guy was willing to accept the provisional articles of peace, he surmised that it was only "to save G Britain's Honor," for Congress was in no position to continue the war. The Pennsylvania line was in mutiny, demanding back pay, and congressmen had fled from Philadelphia to Princeton. "We are on the Eve of a Revolution that will lay aside the Congress and the Republican Models," he predicted to Sir Guy, and "the Change will be either the setting up of the British model with a Reunion, or with a *new King.*" It was clear that he meant a different King George, surnamed Washington.

There seemed less harmony among the thirteen states than

between Carleton and Washington. Dividing the welcoming apple was almost symbolic of the times. There was less and less to share as the army downsized by order of the penurious Congress. To provision his few troops marching to New York from West Point, Washington had to beg Governor Clinton for £2,000. When Clinton claimed he had less than that in his treasury, offering only £1,700—when he could find even that much—Washington's harried Quartermaster General Timothy Pickering called on Robert Morris in Philadelphia for whatever funds could be furnished immediately. But *immediately* meant a delay of days, for a hundred miles in either direction was an arduous journey in the best of times. He was "truly sorry," Morris replied, "that the States are inattentive to the Finances of the Union."

Washington was openly bitter about the reluctance of the weakly confederated former colonies to bear the burden of their own self-interest. As he wrote to James McHenry, a member of Congress from Maryland (for whom the fort was named over which the "Star-Spangled Banner" of the national anthem would be flown in the War of 1812), the states were "very nearly the ruin of our cause." With the war, but not its accumulated problems, over, "It really appears, from the conduct of the States, that they do not conceive it necessary for the Army to receive anything but hard knocks; to give them pay is a matter wch. has been long out of the question and we were upon the very point of trying our hand at how we could live without subsistence. . . . Our Horses have long been without every thing their own thriftiness could not supply. Let any Man, who will allow reason fair play, ask himself what must be the inevitable consequences of such policy. Have not Military Men the same feelings as those in [the] Civil line?" While the soldier endured a litany of hardships, Washington reminded McHenry, "the

Man in civil life sits quiet under his own vine and fig tree solacing himself in all the comforts, pleasures and enjoyments of life. . . ."*

The stocky, graying Morris, official financier of the revolution under some title or other since 1778, was an improviser almost always up to an emergency. He had emigrated with his parents to Pennsylvania from Liverpool at thirteen, rising from messenger in a counting house to managing partner in Willing, Morris & Co. Although he had cautiously voted against the Declaration of Independence, he quickly came 'round. Soon, as the effective chairman of the executive committee appointed by the Continental Congress, he represented the civil authority behind Washington. Despite the disinterest of the individual states in supporting the rebellion by taxing their citizens, Morris somehow gambled and overextended his authority to secure enough credit to enable Washington's army to survive.

While taking great risks in financing Washington's army, to the resentment of some patriot worthies he continued his own commercial affairs (as did others, like John Hancock), overlooking no opportunity for profit. His "Morris notes" were drafts against him secured by his ability to pay, privately or with government allocations, at periods from thirty to sixty days, and their credibility rested on his making them good. But a decade after the war his overextended personal finances collapsed, and the one-time merchant prince would spend more than three

---

*Apparently Washington's favorite scriptural phrase, it came from 1 Kings 4:25: "Judah and Israel dwelt safely, every man under his vine and under his fig tree." In 1797, just before his second and final retirement, Martha Washington thanked John Trumbull for a "proof print" of his portrait of her husband, adding that "a few weeks now, will place me in the shades of Mount Vernon, under our own vines and fig trees. . . ." Almost certainly Mrs. Washington, not much of a letter writer, penned the acknowledgment, full of familiar echoes, to the President's dictation.

years in a debtors' prison at Cherry Hill. In his last years, reduced to a small house in Philadelphia, he lived quietly on an
annuity secured for his wife.

En route to New York, the Continentals encamped nightly
north of the city, often in rain and wet snow, each day a little
closer to their goal. A silent and sullen British rear guard
waited for orders from Carleton to withdraw by stages. Some
troops were not even told of the final evacuation. As Hessian
Lieutenant Carl von Kraaft, a Saxon of thirty-one who had been
in America since 1776, noted in his diary on the nineteenth,
"We now had definite orders to be embarked by noon of Friday
[November 21st], but this was kept secret from the privates to
avoid desertion." He had already readied himself for the voyage
by buying a young pig at Keyser's slaughterhouse for four Span-
ish dollars and had sausages made from it and salted for smoking.

Despite his careful preparations for many weeks at sea,
Kraaft fancied desertion himself. He had been married secretly
earlier in the year to Cornelia de la Metre, who lived with her
widowed mother "past the 5th Mile Stone, King's Bridge Road."
Many Hessians planned to remain—or return. "My heart is full
of sadness," Kraaft would soon write, "when I see fading from
my view the receding landmarks and house-tops, in whose
midst I leave my whole happiness behind me." He never referred to Cornelia. Someone inappropriate might find his diary.
(Although he returned to England according to his orders, he
would sail back in February to be present at the baptism of his
eldest son, Cornelius Frederick, on April 30, 1784.)

America seemed utopian to many Germans, but desertion
came at a heavy price if the escapees were caught and returned.
Officially the sentence was death, but court martial discipline
was usually mitigated by commanders to "running the gantlet

30 times through 200 men on 3 [successive] days." Death might have been preferable.

On November 19, Sir Guy had sent a new message on arrangements to Washington, again with his senior intelligence officer, Major George Beckwith, intermediary with General Benedict Arnold in his treason after Major John André had been captured and executed. Weather conditions offshore continued to delay the sailings. Carleton still hoped to "retire" from the northern approaches to the city on November 21, but his earlier schedule was now, he confessed, "impracticable." Although the winds had become "very unfavorable," he observed through Beckwith, if he had Washington's "assurances that we shall retain a free and uninterrupted use of the Ship-yard and Hallet's Wharf in New York, and the Brewery and Bake-house on Long Island . . . until we can be ready to take our final departure, I shall retire from this city and from Brooklyn on Tuesday next [November 25th] at noon, or as soon after as wind and weather may permit. . . ." (The Brewery and Bakery had been commandeered as a warehouse for goods to be loaded and as a hospital for "sick seamen.")

Until the last redcoats sailed, Sir Guy expected to retain "Staten Island, with Dennis's [Ferry], New Utrecht, and the circumjacent district on Long Island, for such time as may be found absolutely requisite for the troops that may then remain unprovided with transports." Although he was an efficient organizer, he had years of occupation to undo, with ships too undersized and too few for his needs. Washington understood, and replied accommodatingly via Beckwith, who was now acceptable despite his past, that the needed dispositions would be made in concert with Clinton "at the times therein specified." The General dismissed Carleton's warning that as he withdrew, widespread looting might occur. That "a deliberate combination" existed "to plunder the city of New York," so Washington disputed politely through the waiting courier, " . . . appears to me not to be well-founded." He claimed to have "good intelligence" in the city and that "such arrangements have been made, as will, in my opinion, not only utterly discountenance, but effectually prevent, any outrage or disorder."

On Friday November 21, the senior American staff trotting south from West Point dismounted at the Widow Day's tavern in the village of Harlem, nine miles north of the city, near the present 125th Street and Eighth Avenue. Despite colorful identifying signs advertising ale, taverns were also coach stops, watering places for horses, small overnight hotels, and all-purpose meeting points. Washington's arrival at Day's to await his troops and to hold a council was no secret. Celebratory flags fluttered from nearby houses, happy onlookers awaited the patriot party, and Sir Guy Carleton's headquarters was apprised of the General's plans.

Unfortunately also waiting—according to an acerbic press account—was the "humane and polite" Captain William Cunningham, brandishing his familiar bullwhip, who arrived "at the head of a party of British Hannibals in all the pomp of a military parade." It was quite unlikely that the tall, ruddy, and insolent Cunningham, who "wore his hair tied in a cue, with powdered bat-wings over his ears," and was identified as *le Bourreau General* (the official hangman) acted under any orders but his own. As the provost marshal, in charge of prisons and executions, he had ordered to the gallows many inmates held in filthy warehouses and dismasted ships who had not expired soon enough to suit him.

According to a press account, "*Monsieur le Bourreau* . . . having pronounced some scores of double-headed damns, besides the genteel epithets of rebel bitches, &c., without number [obviously directed at Mrs. Day], in the true Milesian cadence, proceeded, with his party, *faire la main,* to tear down the obnoxious [American] colours, and carried them to his den, where it is said they were hoisted [insultingly] with the British colours over them." (The slur referred to the Irish, the rude descendants of the mythical King Milesius, alleged conqueror of Ireland in 1300 B.C.)

A variant of the newspaper's report had the coarse, swaggering Cunningham ripping down every Stars and Stripes he could discover in Harlem, until he reached Day's Tavern. There, while onlookers cheered his comeuppance, the formidable Mrs. Day routed him as he reached for her flag, hammering her stick at Cunningham until powder sprayed from his wig. He beat a retreat from Mrs. Day's bludgeon still carrying plunder looted earlier.*

Another occupation incident occurred when "a fracas happened" at a coffeehouse. An American officer was insulted by a departing "son of Bellona" (Bellona was the Roman goddess of war). According to the press account, the American reached for his horsewhip, with which he administered "about half a dozen *coups de pieds au derriere.*" Other Englishmen did not intervene.

At Mrs. Day's, Washington received a message from Carleton that shipping problems still held him. The fleet of twenty transports, escorted by the frigate *Astrea,* that had evacuated an earlier contingent of soldiers and civilians to Halifax and had just returned to Sandy Hook, had not yet been reprovisioned "on account of the badness of the weather." Although the twenty-third was a Sunday, the little-observed Sabbath did not keep Carleton's men from loading their transports as they

---

*In a reversal of position for him, Cunningham, who left New York with other redcoats, was hanged at Newgate Prison in London for forgery on August 10, 1791.

could. In the rain, the Continentals inched closer, encamping at McGowan's Pass, now the northern border of Central Park at 110th Street. American pickets moved even farther south, to Dove Tavern, on the old post road near the present 65th Street.

The next day, November 24, as the clouds cleared, a dispatch rider brought word that Sir Guy and his rear guard would finally be gone from New York Island by the next noon, and "the Committee appointed to conduct the Order of Receiving their Excellencies Governor Clinton and General Washington," freely operating with the city, issued its instructions for a line of march, soon distributed widely on handbills. Poles, shop windows, hoardings, and even brick walls displayed the notices. There was no British interference.

At McGowan's Pass, Colonel Henry Jackson of Massachusetts issued his orders. "The troops will cook one day's provisions this evening, and be in perfect readiness to march to-morrow morning at 8 o'clock. . . . As soon as the Troops are form'd in the City, the main guard will be march'd off to Fort George—on their taking possession an officer of Artillery will immediately hoist the American standard." He ordered thirteen rounds fired at the flag-raising, and another thirteen when Washington and Clinton passed. "In case of any disturbance the whole of the Patroles will instantly march out, preserve the peace, and apprehend and secure all defenders," including "any violent and disorderly soldiers they may meet with."

There would be little need for such precautions. Only token sentinels remained, with a few redcoat officers supervising. Everyone else evacuating the city was moving toward the Battery docks in good order. It was as if the enemy had already left.

4

REOCCUPATION

On November 25, 1783, a breezy morning with a cold yet bright sun, the final march of Washington's dwindling army—less than eight hundred men commanded by Colonel Jackson—began. Only a month remained until Christmas. (When the Marquis de Lafayette heard of the progress to New York many weeks later, he wrote from Paris of his surprise that the army had been "disbanded" but for "a peace Establishement of 800 men." By then there were even fewer.) The foot soldiers, eight abreast, were from the Massachusetts line and the artillerymen from New York, as all other units north of the Potomac had been ordered home except a frontier garrison at Fort Pitt, the future Pittsburgh.

The takeover by Washington's few seemed shameful to the departing British troops. They had not only occupied New York since early in the revolution but had never been driven out. They had also remained for the two years of no war–no peace since the surrender of Lord Cornwallis and his army in Virginia. Until the evacuation began, twelve thousand of the King's men had sat uselessly in New York garrisons doing little more than deny the city to the enemy. What troops were left were now relinquishing New York to Washington's handful, who could never have fought their way in.

He had won by not losing. As Claude Robin wrote in his letters to France, Washington's reputation had "at length risen to a most brilliant pitch; and he may now exercise almost unbounded power, without provoking envy, or exciting suspicion. He has ever shown himself superior to fortune, and, in the most trying adversity, has discovered resources till then unknown . . . , as if his abilities only increased and dilated at the prospect of difficulty." The Abbé perceived the General's success as the ability to exploit weakness, as he was indeed doing in reoccupying New York with his few troops. Washington, so Robin observed, "has always found means to conceal the real number [of his troops], even from those who compose it." And, "like Peter the Great, he has by defeats conducted his army to victory; and, like [Quintus] Fabius (but with fewer resources, and more difficulty) he has conquered without frequent battles, and saved his country."*

Committees of staunch Americans in the city were displaying previously concealed flags and conducting volunteer patrols, even after dark, to maintain order. Newspapers advised that army veterans wear identifying union cockades of black-and-white "ribands" on the left breast, with sprigs of laurel in their hats. "The Committee hope," its handbill cautioned, "to

---

*Quintus Fabius Maximus, the Roman consul elected dictator in 217 A.D., was known as *Cunctator,* the delayer. Avoiding great battles in the Second Punic War, he conserved his forces and employed them frugally—and successfully. The image had been used as early as 1778, by artist-poet (and army officer) John Trumbull, who wrote of Washington's "Fabian art, victorious by delay."

see their Fellow-Citizens conduct themselves with Decency and Decorum on this joyful Occasion."

The soldiers themselves marched proudly although far from fashionably in their worn, and far from warm, motley garb. Few had sturdy coats, and fewer had gloves. Bearing themselves less proudly were troops they had left farther up the Hudson, near Saratoga, to all intents and purposes discharged. Lieutenant Jeremiah Greenman, of an upstate contingent, noted in his diary (he had learned to read and write in the army, and to keep rolls and accounts) that two British officers on horseback heading north to Canada informed them that the "Definitive Treaty" had arrived at New York. Still, Greenman wrote, his men were "continuing in Garrison waiting anxiously for [the] Order to leave this post, our men in a Miserable Condition. Some of them [have] not a Shoe or a Stocking to their feet and the climate at this place [is] much sevearer, than in the E[a]stern States." He had enlisted from Rhode Island. He knew what a Continental recruit's life was like, having risen from private soldier at seventeen.

The British had left a token barrier on Bowery Lane, near Grand Street, toward which Washington, Clinton, and the accompanying guard of honor—hardly an army any longer—trooped down the Boston Post Road, now bare of fences and dense treeline. The departing occupiers had stripped timber of every sort to feed their garrison fires. The terrain no longer appeared as it had the last time Washington had ridden through, but he could not help remembering how, seven years earlier, it was the scene of one of his worst days in the war. On a clear, cold morning in mid-September 1776, a phalanx of enemy frigates in the East River and another fleet in the Hudson had bombarded the raw, poorly trained, and inadequately armed Continentals in Manhattan. Then, under the roar and smoke of covering grapeshot fire in Kip's Bay, the British had landed a small contingent from the Brooklyn side.

However erratic, enemy cannon had panicked the green troops. Terrified volunteers abandoned their positions as Washington galloped hastily from his headquarters in Harlem. As he neared, he realized to his "surprise and mortification" that his men—soldiers in little more than name—were "retreating with the utmost precipitation, . . . flying in every direction and in the utmost confusion, notwithstanding the efforts of their generals to form them." With sword drawn and high on horseback, conspicuously vulnerable himself, Washington had employed "every means in my power to rally and get them in order," he remembered, "but my efforts were fruitless and ineffectual, and on the appearance of a small party of the enemy, not more than sixty or seventy in number, their disorder increased, and they ran away without firing a shot."

It had been a "disgraceful and dastardly" performance. In his fury he lost his composure, striking at several officers he found running away and throwing his hat to the ground. "Good God," a nearby officer heard him shout, "have I got such troops as these?" Another recalled his raging, "Are these the men with whom I am to defend America?" It was a humiliating experience, and he would have more such days—and years.

Whatever the reasons (very likely inadequate field leadership, as the Americans had no professional officer corps), the demoralized foot soldiers, many under fire for the first time, had taken fright and fled from their ditches and barricades. Improvising a retreat north to Harlem Heights, General Israel Putnam had his men carry off provisions and ammunition, abandoning precious but less portable artillery. Paralyzed by the debacle, Washington lingered until an aide clutched at the bridle of the General's horse and pulled him away before he was captured by Howe's advancing troops.

Although one of Washington's few reliable colonels, Thomas Knowlton, was killed in a skirmish the next day, General Howe preferred caution to following up the rout of the day before. For the moment the Americans kept the high ground, but this was the last time Washington had set foot in Manhattan—York Island to the British. Now everything had changed, and Washington was ostensibly Governor Clinton's guest in a city nearly emptied of an undefeated enemy.

An anonymous versifier penned an overcharged ode celebrating the occasion, printed on handbills and to be sung to the melody of the then familiar Moravian hymn, "He Comes! He Comes with a Trumpet Sound!":

> They come! They come! The Heroes come
> With sounding fife, and thund'ring drum.
> Their ranks advance in bright array,
> The Heroes of AMERICA.
> He comes! 'Tis mighty WASHINGTON!
> Words fail to tell all he has done;
> Our Hero, Guardian, Father, Friend!
> His fame can never, never end. . . .
> Now Freedom has our withers crown'd
> Let flowing goblets pass around:
> We'll drink to Freedom's fav'rite Son,
> Health, Peace & Joy to WASHINGTON!

For the most part, decorum prevailed, but loyalist printer and bookseller James Rivington was too notorious to evade his comeuppance. Rivington's *Royal Gazette,* soon to undergo a prudent masthead reversal, had its premises stoned after perversely characterizing Washington as "the murderer of [convicted spy John] André." Benjamin Tallmadge had been sent into New York not only to parley with Carleton but also to attempt to protect citizens like the publisher, who had managed a double life since 1781, behaving like a Tory while slipping information to Washington bound into books purchased by his spies. One of the bards of the Revolution, Philip Freneau, in a satire, "Rivington's Reflections," would explain, supposedly in the guilty editor's voice,

> *For what have I done when we come to consider,*
> *But sold my commodities to the best bidder?*
> *If I offered to lie for the sake of a post,*
> *Was I to blame if the king offered most?*

Freneau never knew that the highest bidder, with Morris's coin, was Washington. The once jolly, high-living Rivington would expunge the royal arms from his paper and change its name to *Rivington's New York Gazette and Universal Advertiser,* but the loyalist stigma remained. As the *New Hampshire Gazette* would report, "That obnoxious, Jesuitical Printer, James Rivington, who has seldom been seen in the streets since the abdication of his friends the British, was met yesterday by Mr. Cruger, a few paces from his own door, who disciplined him very handsomely for some of his meritorious actions in the reign of George the Third." It was only a mild rebuke, but Rivington would have to cease publication at the end of December and struggle afterward to hang on as a bookseller and stationer. Thanks to his covert earnings from supplying intelligence to the Rebels he was able to live on in New York in relative comfort until he died at 78 in 1802.

At the Bull's Head Tavern, between Bayard Street and Pump (now part of Canal) Street, troops waited for the return of the formidable General Knox, who had ridden ahead toward Bowl-

ing Green to reconnoiter "at the lower end of the Broad Way."
There he would rendezvous and return with a mounted contingent of New Yorkers, four abreast, via Chatham Street. Some
had already been restored to their homes and businesses; others had lain low under the occupation; still others were officers
retired since Yorktown. With them were happy citizens walking
eight abreast, forming a further column to continue the march.
In all their hats were identifying sprigs of laurel. Decades later
a Roxbury, Massachusetts resident recalled how the "large concourse of citizens on horseback and on foot, in plain dress," appeared, "an interesting sight to those of mature age who were
capable of comprehending their merit. In their ranks were seen
men with patched elbows, odd buttons on their coats, and un-
matched buckles on their shoes; they were not indeed Falstaff's
company of scare-crows, but most respectable citizens, who
had been in exile and endured privations we know not of, for
seven long and tedious years."

Pausing briefly at the tavern where a bull's head sign dan-
gled from a pole, Washington and Clinton were served glasses
of ale by the Bull's Head landlord. The throng outside waited
patiently. Then, remounting his warhorse Nelson, a handsome
gray stallion, Washington, with Clinton at his side on a bay
gelding, signaled their escorts to move on. Cantering ahead
were the Westchester Light Dragoons of the local militia, in
civilian garb like Washington and Clinton—a symbolic gesture
to suggest peace rather than war. When the vanguard reached
the present Cooper Square, then the northern boundary of the
city, the column again halted briefly. They had arrived too soon.
They rested on the grass until one o'clock, their prearranged
entry time.

Crowds cheered as the Continentals proceeded to the Tea
Water Pump at Fresh Water in Chatham Street, where, after a

pause for handshakings and rounds of congratulations, the burgeoning party re-formed, but without Knox and his aides. Passing the corner of William Street while their drums beat a march, the troops looked up silently at the mutilated statue of the hawk-nosed Earl of Chatham, who had thundered in Parliament when still William Pitt, "I rejoice that America has resisted. Three millions of people so dead to all feelings of liberty as voluntarily to submit to be slaves would have been fit instruments to make slaves of the rest."

While the ranks and the civilians paraded down Broadway, Knox had trotted on to the next station, Cape's Tavern, already the scene of hardly interrupted enthusiasm for several days, once it became known that it would be a stopping place for Washington. It had been the city residence of Governor DeLancey long before the war and was on the major road south to the ferries. In 1754, Edward Willett had taken over the building as a tavern site and opened under the sign of the Province Arms. Soon it was the York Arms, then the City Arms and the State Arms. By the end of the war it was merely Cape's.

The Continentals came. "We had been accustomed for a long time," a young woman watching along Broadway recalled, "to military display in all the finish and finery of garrison life; the [British] troops just leaving us were as if equipped for show, and with their scarlet uniforms and burnished arms, made a brilliant display; the troops that marched in, on the contrary, were ill-clad and weather beaten, and made a forlorn appearance; but then they were *our* troops, and as I looked at them and thought upon all they had done and suffered for us, my heart and my eyes were full, and I admired and gloried in them the more, because they were weather beaten and forlorn."

Although they looked shabby compared with the smartly garbed British and Hessians, they seemed to Washington proud and (relatively) spruce. He remembered Kip's Bay in 1776 and Valley Forge in 1777–1778.

At the entrance to Cape's, Washington received homage from local dignitaries crowding about, eager to be part of the occasion. As courteous as he was tireless, the General was a patient listener. There would be many more felicitations to endure through the week.

The column moved slowly as throngs clotting the streets cheered, then moved back to let the Continentals pass. As troops reached the country house of James William Beekman, near the present 51st Street and First Avenue, with a greensward that sloped down to the banks of the East River, some officers with their staffs and a few invited civilians halted the march long enough to be "entertained in its drawing-room with punch made with lemons plucked from trees growing in the green-house." Some New Yorkers had lived grandly—and safely—under whatever flag flew. Many exiles with once imposing properties now found their holdings less so. James Duane, who repossessed his houses on King Street and Water Street, discovered their interiors "almost entirely destroyed," but his farm, twenty acres and now part of Gramercy Park, was in better condition, having been occupied by a British general. Many public buildings fared poorly. Under military rule, all churches except those of the Anglican, Methodist, and Moravian denominations had been stripped of pews and pulpits, and converted into prisons, riding halls, hospitals, barracks, and storehouses. Only the Dutch church in Garden Street was in good enough condition to be reopened on the first Sunday after the evacuation. (Not being a church, the Shearith Israel synagogue, founded by twenty-six Jews who arrived in Peter Stuyvesant's day aboard a French privateer from Brazil to live in New Netherland, had survived.)

At one o'clock the British officer in charge of "the barrier"—the Bowery gateway at the line of Grand Street—formally delivered the barricade to General Knox. The remaining redcoats retired stiffly toward the wharves, down what was still called the King's Highway, an anachronism that lingers on in Brooklyn, in King's County.

Until that morning, Fort George, on the Battery, its name derived from the first cannon there, in 1693, had been the official residence of the Provincial Governor. (To its east was Whitehall Slip, with Bowling Green above. Only later was the Battery area enlarged with landfill.) Above the northern rampart of the outworks of the high stone fortress, a bare flagpole attracted watchers. On closer inspection it became obvious that no Stars and Stripes could be raised. When the British had lowered the Union Jack for the last time, they had meanly cut the halyards. With no hoist to employ, lifting a flag to the top required shinnying up the shaft—yet as further parting devilry, sly redcoats had greased the pole.

From out in the bay, sailors on small boats going out to the last ships in the harbor rested on their oars and watched as a volunteer tried to scale the flagstaff. If British tars jeered scornfully, they were too distant to be heard.

Early in the war, Washington had flown the Grand Union flag, with the now familiar thirteen red and white stripes for the thirteen colonies. In its topmost quarter near the staff was the Union Jack. After the severing of ties with Britain, the new flag authorized by Congress substituted a circlet of thirteen white stars on a blue field, described as "a new constellation." To fly it over Fort George, the Clinton Papers explain, "We were obliged to have a ladder [fetched] to fix a new rope. . . . [Meanwhile,] the glorious stripes were fixed [on an improvised pole] in the sod, and a discharge of thirteen [muskets] fired." The last of the British evacuees again laid on their oars, and the throng of gawkers that had followed soldiers to the enticing flagpole disconsolately made its way back to Cape's Tavern.

Some patriots shouted their dissatisfaction. American pride required something better. As John Van Dyck, then a boy, later a naval captain, recalled forty-eight years later, "I was on Fort George, and within two feet of the flag staff. The halyards were unreeved [by the redcoats], the cleats were knocked off, the flag staff was slushed, and a sailor boy (not a man) tried three times [to climb the pole], and got up about three feet when he slipped down." Emergency measures were called for. "Some persons ran to Mr. Golet's, [the] iron monger, in Hanover Square . . . , and got a hand saw, hatchet, gimblets, and nails; one sawed lengths across the board, one split the cleats, and some bored, until they had plenty of them. The sailor boy tied the halyards around his waist, filled his outside sailor jacket pockets full of the cleats, then began to nail them on from the ground, on the right and left of the flag staff; as he ascended . . . he nailed the cleats on, then he reeved the halyards, and when the American flag was then hoisted on Fort George, a[nother] salute was fired of 13 rounds . . . and three cheers were given."*

John Trumbull would imagine, in a large painting done from a study in 1790, Washington at Fort George, standing in blue dress coat beside his horse Nelson, seen pawing at the ground. "I represented . . . in the background," he recalled, "a view of Broadway in ruins, as it then was, the old Fort at the termination [of the occupation]; British ships and boats leaving the

---

*Another story, in a pamphlet by James Riker published the same year (1831), claimed that the British had fixed a Union Jack to the top of the pole, then removed any means of getting it down. In Riker's version, John Van Arsdale, the climbing sailor boy, ripped down the British flag when he reached the top. Although the Riker alternative is more melodramatic, very likely the British would have left no flag to be vandalized.

shore, and Staten Island in the distance." Although he claimed to have worked "from the real objects," the scene was entirely a fiction.

Across the East River another reoccupation revel went on in Flatbush, where, Daniel Van Pelt recalled, "gathered all the returned patriots to give emphasis to their joy at their restoration to country and home." Suddenly "two stanch Kings County Whigs hailing from Flatlands" (southeast of Flatbush) turned up. "These were Elias Hubbard and Abraham Voorhees. All that each found . . . on his farm was an old horse blind of one eye. They hitched these two dilapidated animals together to one wagon, and thus drove to Flatbush." Their appearance "created a sensation." Nearby, the innkeeper at the King's Arms had kept his tavern sign from confiscation by adding an American eagle to the royal device, "represented as flying away with the same."

Although the British were supposed to be gone altogether when the Americans arrived, the coffeehouse affair near the Battery suggests that there was some overlap while the last redcoats awaited evacuation. And there would be more. On the first Saturday night the Americans were in the city, a fire broke out at the brewery in Gold Street, near Maiden Lane. The blaze spread furiously, consuming the mansion of retired Colonel Henry Rutgers and several warehouses, and was extinguished only with the help the firemen received from local citizens and some remaining British troops. "The assistance afforded by the British officers and soldiers," a newspaper observed, "does them singular honor. [The fire] is supposed to have been perpetrated by some discontented person or persons of the Refugee complexion."

Watching from shipboard, Lieutenant Kraaft noted in his diary that although New York was "full of Rebels," the "watches" on duty were still English, and the fire, which began soon after eleven, "continued until 3 in the morning, when we could see no more." The "ringing of alarm bells and the uproar made by the disgustingly drunken sailors of our ship who had been in the city until late, made it quite a restless night."

More than a new fire contributed to the devastation in the decaying city of twenty-one thousand. There had been great fires in 1776 and 1778, and little rebuilding. Streets and sidewalks remained in disrepair; broken street lamps had not been replaced; wharves and warehouses not used by the occupiers had been neglected; and as evacuation time approached, neglected dirt and rubbish piled up, including dead animals left in the streets or dumped into canals. Hogs rooted in Bowling Green, once the lively focus of the city's life. (Roaming hogs were a curious feature of many American cities until reformers got rid of them in the mid-1840s.) Across Broad Street and extending southward to Old Slip, an improvised settlement called Canvas Town had emerged amid the ruins left by the second great fire.

British indifference to the condition of New York had already caused controversy among the returned exiles. Fighting about retribution and banishment, General Alexander McDougall, a New Yorker and prewar leader of the local Sons of Liberty, argued for law and order with the irate William Malcolm, a returned municipal official who wanted vigilante action to drive the Tories who remained out of the city. With commerce in a shambles, anyone who would rebuild seemed useful to have about.

On the evening of the twenty-fifth at Cape's, harmony reigned, as Governor Clinton presided at a convivial public dinner for Washington, his officers, and three hundred of patriot New York's "Gentlemen"—all the inn could hold. The banquet was sponsored by the returned New York exiles. Wine was plentiful, and the evening "was spent in great good Humor, Hilarity and Mirth, becoming the joyous occasion." There were thirteen symbolic toasts, opening with the new nation, the French king, the Netherlands, the king of Sweden, the American army, and the fleet and army of France. Then came, as toasts seven to thirteen,

> *The memory of those heroes who have fallen for our Freedom.*
> *May our country be grateful to her military children.*
> *May justice support what courage has gained.*
> *The vindicators of the rights of mankind in every quarter of the globe.*
> *May America be an asylum to the persecuted of the earth.*
> *May a close union of the states guard the temple they have erected to Liberty.*
> *May the remembrance of THIS DAY be a lesson to Princes.*

Following the toasts came a compliment to Governor Clinton from the organizers for his "faithful labours at the head of the government of this State." His response was that New Yorkers had to show, by their virtues, "that we deserve to partake of the freedom, sovereignty and independence, which are so happily established throughout these United States."

Washington was then offered "salutations" in the name of "long suffering exiles, but now happy freemen," who, looking ahead to their "deliverer's" retirement, hoped "that the cries of injured liberty may never more interrupt your repose; and that your happiness may be equal to your virtues." The General's reply seemed too pompous to be anything but the hastily ghostwritten prose of one of his busy aides. "May the tranquility of your city be perpetual," he closed, standing tall and stately. "May the ruins soon be repaired, commerce flourish, science be fostered, and all the civil and social virtues be cherished, in the same illustrious manner which formerly reflected so much credit on the inhabitants of New York."

Leaving the city for his evacuation ship, the Reverend Ewald Schaukirk, a Hessian chaplain, recalled in his diary, "On all corners one saw the flag of thirteen stripes flying, cannon salutes were fired, and all the bells rang. The shores were crowded with people who threw their hats in the air, screaming and boisterous with joy, and wished us a pleasant voyage with white handkerchiefs. . . . On the ships, which lay at anchor with the troops, a deep stillness prevailed as if everyone were mourning the loss of the thirteen beautiful provinces." At ten that night, under cover of darkness, Sir Guy Carleton's own frigate, HMS *Ceres*, with other ships to sail for Plymouth or Portsmouth, and lying off New York harbor, moved away quietly to anchor off Staten Island and await favorable winds. With him were leading area Tories. Lesser departing "Gentlemen"—the term applied by James Rivington's *Gazette*—were accommodated in the *Cyclops*. "His Majesty's troops and such remaining Loyalists as chose to emigrate," Carleton claimed to Lord North in London, "were successfully withdrawn on the 25th . . . from the city of New York in good order, and embarked without the smallest circumstance of irregularity or misbehaviour of any kind." Some civilians had left behind their families, as only those provable as British accomplices were at risk, and property likely to be confiscated might, if lived in, remain secure.

One such official embarking with Carleton was his close associate, William Smith, who had become Chief Justice for the province of New York under the Tory governor William Tryon. His hopes for reunion gone, Smith had made his will on November 16, leaving his considerable fortune to his wife, Janet, and their four children, while stubbornly referring to their residence on lower Broadway as in "the Colony of New York"—as it no longer was. Until the *Ceres* actually left the harbor behind, he and others on board would be able send messages to the mainland. No local authority attempted to control the small boats—"conveyances," Smith called them—that swarmed about in the choppy water seeking small change for such services.

The next morning, according to the memoir of Washington by Martha's grandson George Washington Parke Custis, the only source for the occasion, the General walked to No. 23 Queen Street (now 218 Pearl Street) with several of his staff to breakfast with the family of Hercules Mulligan, a prominent haberdasher of large proportions, "to the wonder of the Tories and the perfect horror of the Whigs." If the General did, it was to acknowledge personally the help of Mulligan as an informer on the British. Six years later when back in the city, Washington would patronize the Irishman's expensive establishment. Although he then paid for the merchandise, it is unknown whether he paid earlier for Mulligan's very different services. His relationships with apparent Tories in New York, like Rivington and Mulligan, during the gala week remained curious. Once in the city he received a letter from a prominent local Royalist, Andrew Elliot, who was already aboard an evacuation ship in the harbor, asking that the General look after Elliot's daughter, Mrs. Eleanor Jauncey. Washington visited the lady and offered to render any service. "I am confident, Sir," the Commander-in-Chief wrote to Elliot in a message delivered by a courier who was rowed out to the British transport ". . .that the most perfect regularity and good order prevail in this city, and that every description of People find themselves under the protection of the Laws of the State." Elliot was not to worry about his daughter but why Washington had made the unusual social call remains a mystery. Perhaps Elliot, too, served both sides.

Washington did not know, and would have been embarrassed had he seen it, that on the morning after his visit to Mulligan, November 26, the *Freeman's Journal* in Philadelphia had published a satiric piece glorifying him, tongue-in-cheek. For nearly two centuries the former colonies had been subject to a monarch and an aristocracy, and it was not uncommon for Americans to think of Washington in such terms, while his plump but tiny spouse, always elegant in dress and manners, was often referred to as "Lady Washington." In some ways, Martha acted queenly, although as a Dandridge her family did not even rate a coat of arms. She had written from Newburgh that February of having been at her husband's pardoning ceremony of all remaining military prisoners. "They had come in a body. One of them was spokesman for the rest. My heart was touched and my eyes were filled with tears. I gave the speaker some money to divide among them all, and bade them 'go, and sin no more.' The poor fellow kissed my hand and said 'God bless Lady Washington.'"

On August 7, congressmen at Princeton (with ten states present) had resolved "That an equestrian statue of General Washington, should be erected in the place where the residence of Congress shall be established." Further, "That the statue be of bronze: the General to be represented in a Roman dress, holding a truncheon in his right hand, and his head encircled with a laurel wreath: the statue to be supported by a marble pedestal, on which are to be represented, in basso relievo, the . . . principal events of the war, in which General Washington commanded in person. . . ." There was not even a modest protest from Washington, who, on August 26, 1783, attended Congress himself, received its congratulations, and responded with his "deepest feelings of gratitude." There was enough of the aristocrat in him to accept the honor as his due, but it would be decades before such recognition materialized, and even then the concept had to be rescued from fantasy. Robert Mills's design of the 1840s for a soaring granite obelisk included, at the top, the figure of a Roman Washington in a triumphal chariot.

In October, Congress voted to site the capital on the banks of the Delaware near Trenton, then backtracked when southerners objected. As there was no "general assent to any one place," Elbridge Gerry of Massachusetts moved in Solomonic if impractical fashion that "the alternative residence of Congress in two places" would be useful in "securing the mutual confidence and affections of the states, and preserving the balance of power." His proposal, promoted also by Thomas Jefferson, was to situate a second federal town on the Potomac, near Washington's seat at Mount Vernon. In the interim, while both capitals were designed and built, Congress would reside in alternative six month cycles at Trenton and Annapolis, ensuring that, in Elias Boudinot's metaphor, "we are to be in future wandering Stars and have our Aphelion and Perihelion."*

The motion passed by seven states to four. The matter of the great Washington statue remained unsettled, inspiring Francis Hopkinson's satiric "A Summary of Some Late Proceedings in a Certain Great Assembly," in the *Freeman's Journal*. Imagining jocularly how the issue might be resolved, Hopkin-

---

*The Earth's closest distance to the Sun is its *perihelion*; its most distant point in its only faintly eccentric orbit about the Sun is its *aphelion*. The terms were introduced by pre-Newtonian astronomer Johannes Kepler in 1596. The portly Boudinot, a Presbyterian worthy, had been Commissary General of Prisoners of War for Washington and was then president of the Congress for a one year term.

son, a clever Philadelphia lawyer, poet, and composer, quoted
the supposed address of an ingenious (and fictional) member of
Congress. Well versed in the Homeric saga of Troy, he proposed
a majestic mobile statue of Washington. On wheels, it would be
capacious enough to be "adjourned" from one capital to another while transporting all the congressmen inside. The body
of the horse, if constructed like the hull of a ship, could convey
the members, while the papers of Congress could be archived—
he explained politely—in the horse's rectum.

Further, another fictional member suggested, the cost of
construction of two capitals could be circumvented by building
only one "imperial city" and putting it on wheels, like the
heroic representation of Washington, to move between the
Delaware and the Potomac. There was nothing absurd in the
scheme, he insisted, as nature had furnished examples on a
smaller scale in the portable houses of the snail and the tor-
toise.

Producing a copy of Cyrano de Bergerac's century-old fantasy *A Voyage to the Moon,* he then read dramatically a description of the manner in which an entire city, built on wheels,
equipped with sails, and propelled by bellows, had been moved
at the rate of a hundred leagues in eight days. "The House was
astonished at the extensive genius of the projecting member;
and immediately adjourned; having first recommended it to
each other to consider against the next meeting, if any objections could possibly be made. . . ."

Not all futuristic suggestions about locomotion were in the
realm of fantasy. Intrepid Frenchmen were already lifting off the
ground in hot-air balloons, as Benjamin Franklin had written
with enthusiasm to William Laurens from Passy on December
6. "Yet I fear," he added, "it will hardly become a common Carriage in my time." Still, as Washington was jolting homeward

on horseback, the Philadelphia merchant and shipping magnate William Bingham, who had enriched himself by outfitting privateers and who had been one of the General's agents conducting espionage in the West Indies, was circulating a pamphlet with a copperplate of an air balloon "constructed for the purpose of accommodating a person who intended to take a long voyage through the regions of the air." Improvements, he speculated, would be made in the system, and it was likely to be turned to "useful purposes":

By the assistance of small air balloons attached to different parts of the human body that will be exactly sufficient to keep it suspended in air, in equilibrium, and with the help of a pair of wings, what can prevent its making a progress through the air with great facility? Will this not be a cheap and easy method of travelling?

Washington himself only learned of it later, writing then to Louis le Bèque du Portail, "I have only news paper Accts. of the Air Balloons, to which I do not know what credence to give; as the Tales related of them are marvellous, and lead us to expect that our friends at Paris; in a little time, will come flying through the air, instead of ploughing the Ocean to get to America."

"Jesting apart," Thomas Jefferson would soon write merrily to Francis Hopkinson, "I think this discovery [of ballooning] may lead to things useful. For instance there is no longer a difficulty how Congress may move backwards & forwards, and your bungling scheme of moving houses and moving towns is quite superseded; we shall soar sublime above the clouds." It was ironic that a rapid transit service for congressional documents between Philadelphia and Princeton—a primitive pony express—was already called "the Flying Machine." Although authentically aerial devices would have been helpful in fording rivers and overflying excessive addresses from citizens, such alternatives were not yet available to hasten Washington to Mount Vernon.

Serious business still remained in New York. Now that Washington had taken possession of the city, he planned to bid farewell to what remained of his army.

November 26–December 3, 1783

5

THE FIRST FAREWELL

Neither Hopkinson's satire nor Bingham's leaflet could have reached New York while Washington was being feted there. Impractical in any case, their fantasies would have been of no account during the week of farewell dinners and eulogies for the General so flattering as likely to have turned even a crowned head. Each formal compliment required a Washingtonian response equal to the goodwill of the functionary who had labored to find the proper balance between approbation and awe. Although the General had kept Lieutenant Colonel David Humphreys scribbling at his side, some replies were later submitted in writing.

The bulky Connecticut-born Humphreys, thirty-one, a former schoolmaster, fancied himself a poet. The General utilized his aide-de-camp's unremarkable talents as a wordsmith to draft letters and speeches—and responses to addresses. When, briefly, an aide to General Nathanael Greene of Rhode Island, Humphreys had published a glorification in verse of the commander in chief, which was no worse than most such efforts but included the excessive lines,

His voice inspir'd, his godlike presence led.
The Britons saw, and from his presence fled.

One month later, Humphreys was transferred to Washington's staff as an additional secretary and scribe, nearly the last of the thirty-two aides-de-camp who served the General at various times during the war. Much later, when recalled to Mount Vernon as a civilian secretary, Humphreys would be asked to prepare a first draft of a presidential inaugural address for Washington. After reading it, the President-elect prudently wrote his own speech.

The godlike aura about Washington would intensify as he continued homeward, enhanced by his statuesque presence and his innate dignity. As early as 1777, an anonymous writer in the *Pennsylvania Journal* had responded to an attack on the General, "If there are spots on his character, they are like the spots in the sun, only discernible by the magnifying powers of a telescope. Had he lived in the days of idolatry, he would have been worshipped like a god." Decades later, as far off as a small Latin American republic, a visitor would ask a peasant about a familiar bust over the portal of his village church. That is "the good Saint George Washington," he explained. "I confess," the tourist reported, "that as I passed this church I felt like taking off my hat, and did it—not because of custom, but because I couldn't help it."

A nineteenth century visitor to the United States saw engravings and lithographs of Washington everywhere and observed, "Every American considers it his sacred duty to have a likeness of Washington in his home, just as we have images of God's saints." Such veneration was not limited to ordinary people. Abraham Lincoln wore a gold ring containing a bit of Washington's coffin. (In 1831 the body had been moved to its present tomb, and fragments of the former casket became cherished keepsakes.) At the inauguration of William McKinley in 1897, the new president wore for the ceremony a ring, like a saint's relic, embedded with strands of Washington's hair, a gift to him from John Hay, who had been Lincoln's secretary.

One of the encomiums to which Washington responded in Manhattan was from the "Ministers, Elders, Deacons and Members of the Reformed German Congregation of New York," to whom he wrote that one of the motives "which induced me to the Field" was the "establishment of Civil and Religious Liberty" in America. To "the freeholders and other inhabitants of King's County," Washington urged that they exemplify "a noble instance of magnanimity" to show "that the Laws do govern, and that the Civil Magistrates are worthy of the highest respect and confidence." To New York's large Irish community he wished "the blessings of equal Liberty." Yet he added the implied admonition, as the Irish were reputed to be a rackety people, "The bosom of America is open to receive not only the Opulent and respectable Stranger, but the oppressed and persecuted of all Nations and Religions; whom we shall welcome to a participation of all our rights and privileges, if by decency and propriety of conduct they appear to merit the enjoyment."

At sea off New York, the weather remained too foul for transports to weigh anchor for an Atlantic crossing. To Lieutenant von Kraaft aboard the *Sally* the winds and water appeared calm, but he noticed on November 26 that the nearest ship of the fourteen transports had taken in most of its sails. Its captain had sensed trouble closing in. That night a storm broke off Sandy Hook, and the *Sally,* captained by the less wary Thomas Potter of London, was driven toward land. By morning on November 27 von Kraaft was violently seasick. On deck "a cow, 4 sheep and two pigs and about 30 fowls were killed owing

to the cruel tossing and pitching of the ship. In our cabin everything went to pieces and was afloat. . . ." He blamed Potter's
negligence.

From the *Ceres*, still close in on November 29, a dreary,
cloudy Saturday, William Smith reported to his wife that everything aboard for the evacuees was going well, and he offered
some parting assurance. "Give yourself not a Moment's uneasi-
ness. Every Comfort is to be found here. . . . There are two State
Rooms in the Cabbin of which I have one. The other is Sir G.
Carleton's. . . . You forgot one of the Blankets but 2 suffice,
there being a very good Coal Fire kept up in the Cabbin. I . . .
rather imagine that as soon as the Transports newly arrived are
equipped, we shall sail directly for Portsmouth." Being well-
connected was useful.

The first vessel to arrive in Philadelphia with the definitive
text of the treaty was the French packet the *Courier de l'Europe*,
which docked on November 29 with John Thaxter, secretary to
John Adams, one of the American peace commissioners, aboard
conveying the precious cargo. Its voyage had begun on September 26. Finding New York still occupied by the British, the
packet detoured to Philadelphia. As in all situations in which it
was crucial for a message to arrive safely, as with British orders
to royal commands in America during the war, multiple sailings
with duplicate papers carried messages across the Atlantic. The
British packet *Lord Hyde*, sailing outward from Falmouth in
Cornwall, was also nearing landfall with the treaty, having left
London on September 30.

Additional Loyalist emigrants kept arriving in New York
harbor to be ferried out on small boats to Sir Guy's transports.
Both the public areas and the few private quarters aboard each
vessel were becoming crowded. Among William Smith's companions were Deane Poyntz, Sir Guy's Paymaster General, and

Brook Walton, the Commissary General. "It is very inconven-
ient to write in a Cabbin," Smith explained, "where five Pens
are scribbling round one Table, and Persons of Business at every
Chair." He was "rejoiced to learn" from a message sent by Janet
via one of the new passengers, "that you have not been alarmed
by any Outrages."

Smith worried that as the American army "grew thin, and
unknown Characters from the Country abounded," law and order in the city would break down. Yet a British officer who also
feared the worst, found the opposite. He hurried from his ship
to retrieve, a newspaper reported, "some effects" he had forgot-
ten, and as he was wearing his uniform, he asked the new city
authorities for protection. Although assured that all was "civil
and tranquil," he was offered a guard, returned unmolested,
and as he was reboarding his ship he commented, "This is a
strange scene indeed! Here, in this city, we have had an army
for more than seven years, and yet could not keep the peace of
it. Scarcely a day or night passed without tumults. Now [that]
we are gone, everything is in quietness and safety. These Americans are a curious, original people; they know how to govern
themselves, but nobody else can govern them."

Despite the apparent placidity of the reoccupation, confirmed by Carleton himself, some emigrants expected the worst
happening to those left behind, and with good reason. On De-
cembeer 13 *The Independent New York Gazette* would publish as a
paid advertisement what was described as

A CARD
The exiled Whigs present their most respectful com-
pliments to Messieurs TORIES, and beg leave to inform
those sticklers for *British* tyranny that with heart-felt satisfaction the late-suffering Whigs find the old proverb

fully verified, "After a storm comes a calm." The Whigs take the liberty to prognosticate that the calm, which the enemies of Columbia enjoy, will ere long be succeeded by a bitter and *neck-breaking hurricane.*

Vessels then taking on important personages of the occupation may have worried about such threats before being rowed out to their ships. They were at sea when the "card" appeared. For the most part the violence would be civil—problems of properties and rents.

On the *Cyclops* and the *Assurance,* royalist officials were planning for their future elsewhere. The *Holderness* held the already busy commissariat department, which the efficient Sir Guy expected to be operational on debarking in Halifax. Shortly the *Assurance* would have its orderly departure interrupted.

By being afloat, Smith apparently missed a minor earthquake that shook both New York and Philadelphia. At 10:15 on Saturday evening, according to newspaper reports, "a smart shock" was felt "in and about" Philadelphia, with a less violent tremor at 1:00 on Sunday morning. In New York at about two, "the inhabitants were alarmed by three successive shocks of an earthquake." People "rose from their beds, and ran into the streets." Houses in Philadelphia were "very sensibly shaken, so that in many the china and pewter . . . were thrown off the shelves, and several persons were waked from their sleep." Birds left their roosts, and cattle milled about, lowing. Nature, it seemed, was paralleling the political earthquake.

Despite the late hour, Robert R. Livingston, of an influential political family already returned to Manhattan, was writing to John Jay, one of the treaty negotiators, in Paris. Jeremiah Platt, a prosperous New York merchant, was about to sail for France, and Livingston wanted him to carry a letter to Jay congratulating him "on an event to which you have so greatly contributed to bring about, the evacuation of this City by the British. . . . Our enemies are hardly more astonished than we ourselves and you will [be] when you hear that we have been here five days without the smallest disturbance." Even "the most obnoxious Royalists" opened their shops "the day after we came in, and Rivington himself goes on as usual." The "race of Tories," Livingston predicted, "will not after all be totally extinct in America. Perhaps by good training, and by crossing the breed frequently, . . .they may be rendered useful animals in a few generations."

As he thanked Jay, also, for French prints received of the ascension of the new "air balls" in Paris, his writing table tottered and he was "alarmed by a very loud rumbling noise accompanied by a tremulous motion of the earth. The family are too alarmed to permit me to add more." And Livingston signed off.

Undeterred by shocks that were less than artillery caliber, Washington slept soundly. On Sunday evening, November 30, at Samuel Fraunces' tavern at Pearl and Broad streets, where he was staying (his bill for his own board and lodging would be £35), the General hosted his own modest "Entertainment" and was charged £8:16:0 for having "sent out" for a dinner of "16 dishes." Built in 1719, the handsome brick building of three and a half stories near the Exchange was already venerable. (The present tavern on the same site, following several fires, is a 1907 reimagining.) "Black Sam" Fraunces operated it as the Queen's Head Tavern. The profile on the pub sign remained that of George III's unidentified consort, Charlotte, but Americans preferred the proprietor's name, and it was Fraunces Tavern despite the royal device.

Some British forces were anchored close enough almost to overhear the revelry in New York, or at least to imagine it ruefully, as local news reached their ships. Most evacuees wished they were already at sail, as the beckoning—and long familiar— roofs and spires of the city remained a tantalizing sight. But the winds had picked up, and obstructed, Judge Smith wrote that Monday, the loading of further frigates. "I fear we shall be detained till the latter End of the Week."

Very likely it was that Monday, December 1, a rare morning without engagements, that Washington proposed to two of his staff, "Suppose, gentlemen, we walk down to Rivington's bookstore; he is said to be a very pleasant kind of fellow."

Although astonished at the suggestion—Rivington's local reputation was scandalous—they agreed to accompany their chief. At the bookshop in Lower Wall Street they were received with great courtesy and ushered into a parlor to the rear. There Rivington proposed to Washington, "Will your Excellency do me the honor to step into the adjoining room for a moment [so] that I may show you a list of the *agricultural* works I am about to order out from London for your special use?"

As both retired farther inside, the two aides wondered how and when the General would have had the opportunity to convey a book order to a Tory shopman. Rivington's invitation was a ruse, although months earlier Washington had actually ordered volumes he had seen offered for sale in a city "gazette" through one of his commissioners to Sir Guy Carleton, Lieutenant Colonel William Stephens Smith. Among them—Washington, who had little formal education, was self-taught in such fashion—were biographies of Peter the Great, Gustavus Adolphus, and Charles XII; the letters of Voltaire; the *Memoirs* of the duc de Sully, Henry IV's financier; and William Robertson's *History of America,* published in Scotland in 1777. One was a book on agriculture, Henry Home's treatise of 1779, published in Dublin, *The Gentleman Farmer: Being an Attempt to Improve AGRI-*

CULTURE by Subjecting it to the Test of RATIONAL PRINCIPLES.
He seemed always to be buying books on farming. Soon after he
inherited Mount Vernon he wrote innocently to London for a
treatise encouragingly titled *A New System of Agriculture: Or a
Speedy Method of Growing Rich.* It did not make him speedily rich.

The door of Rivington's inner room failed to latch shut, and
soon creaked slightly ajar. Through the opening the men heard
what seemed to be the chinking of what they guessed were
purses of gold coins, removed presumably from Washington's
capacious uniform coat and set on Rivington's table. George
Washington Parke Custis described the two purses as "the last
instalment of the price of treason." (Washington's expense accounts as of July 1783 noted, without details, his personal ex-
penditure of $55,145.00 in "Lawful" money since 1775 for
"Secret Intelligence.") On emerging with Washington, the
bookseller plucked three goblets from a shelf and offered his
guests some choice Madeira, which he assured them he had imported himself from a vintner whose wine had earned the plaudits of Sir Henry Clinton and other distinguished bon vivants
among the former elite of the city.

When the three Americans, refreshed, rose to depart, Rivington escorted Washington to the outer door, assuring him
loudly, "Your Excellency may rely upon my special attention being given to *the agricultural works,* which, on their arrival, will be
immediately forwarded to Mount Vernon, where I trust they
will contribute to your gratification amid the shades of domestic retirement."

The dapper, genial King's Printer could hardly have been sus-
pected by royalists of rebel leanings. Although the *Salem Gazette*
in Massachusetts soon after, on December 25, 1783, published as
"an undoubted fact"—but without explanation—that the editor
and bookseller was "protected in person, and in property, by a

guard" as Washington's troops reoccupied New York City and that he "will be allowed to reside in this country, for reasons best known to the great men at [the] helm," the hard knocks he took, literally, early that December obscured his duplicity.

> *I confess, that with shame and contrition opprest,*
> *I sign'd an agreement to go [into exile] with the rest,*

Philip Freneau wrote later in Rivington's voice, but the bookdealer "gave them the slip" and hung on in New York until 1797. Then, at seventy-two, he was sentenced to debtor's prison. He had backed the East India ventures of his two elder sons, and their creditors went after him for £20,000, very likely far more than the "dog cheap bargain"—as Custis would call it—Rivington had earned by spying for Washington.

Later that Monday, while Washington was having yet another convivial dinner at Cape's, a letter was delivered to him from Sir Guy, aboard the *Ceres,* confirming that the frigate *Astrea* had arrived with twenty transports, which he hoped to have returned to sea on the fourth, a Thursday. The next day, Washington responded to Carleton with the hope "that your Excellency, with the Troops under your Orders, may have a safe and pleasant passage." He was putting into practice the magnanimity he had recommended to New Yorkers.*

At Cape's that Tuesday, Washington had dined with the Governor and "upwards of a hundred Gentlemen." The official guest of honor was the Chevalier de la Luzerne, the French ambassador, who had come up from Philadelphia. Again there

---

*On his return Carleton received for his services an annuity of £1,000 a year from Parliament. In 1786 he was granted the title of Lord Dorchester.

were toasts to the French king and the French armed forces, who after 1778 had helped keep the colonies in the war. In variations on the now traditional thirteen toasts Washington now heard night after night, one proposed, "May an uninterrupted Commerce soon repair the Ravages of War." (It did not anticipate the soon to be announced British restrictions on American trade.) Another was optimistic: "May the Spirit of Faction be chained in the Regions of Darkness." At what was ostensibly a banquet for the representatives of France, the twelfth toast ventured, "May the sun of American Liberty spread its influence to the ends of the earth." Six years later that hope would materialize at the Bastille in Paris, unseating the king to whom diners had raised their goblets for the second toast.

Accompanying Luzerne was the new French consul, better known as the author Hector St. John de Crèvecoeur, who had published his *Letters from an American Farmer* the year before. He was a naturalist and farmer who had been arrested by the British and languished in a New York prison before being permitted to sail, with a son, to France in 1780. Returning in November 1783 to become consul, he found his farmhouse burned, his wife dead, and his daughter and second son housed with strangers in Boston. Washington knew nothing yet of Crèvecoeur's tragedy, only that he had brought with him, to the General's delight, a letter from the Marquis de Lafayette, whom Washington loved like a son. After Yorktown, with the war over, Lafayette had returned to his family in France, and Washington would confide to Crèvecoeur that nothing would give him more pleasure than to see "that amiable, disinterested, and patriotic young Nobleman" again.

When Major Pierre-Charles L'Enfant, a French engineer in the American service who would later have a role in laying out the District of Columbia, returned to France, he carried a letter from Washington to Lafayette. The General had requested "many

pieces" of Parisian silverplate for Mount Vernon. "I do not in-
cline," the General wrote, "to send to England (from whence formerly I had all my goods) for any thing I can get upon tolerable
terms elsewhere." What Washington had requested, the details
suggesting Martha's wish list, included "a large Tea-Urn," two
teapots with stands, a coffeepot and stand, a cream pot, a tea
chest, two large trays, two smaller trays, two bread baskets, a set
of coasters, "a Cross or Stand for the centre of the Dining table,"
twelve "salts," eight "Bottle sliders," six large goblets, twelve
candlesticks, three pairs of candle snuffers, and "any thing else
which may be deemed necessary, in any way." If the pieces could
be engraved, he added, "I should be glad to have my arms
thereon, the size of which will, it is to be presumed, be large or
small in proportion to the piece on which it is engraved."

Now he wrote only that he no longer needed the plate. Silverplate, produced by a new alloy process, was available at bargain prices in the city, as many of its wealthiest citizens had to
dispose of excess goods before they boarded vessels taking
them into exile. Stowage was limited. The largest frigates and
transports, no larger than a modern ferryboat, each carried
about thirty thousand square feet of flax canvas and miles of
cordage and required nearly three thousand oaks to construct
them, yet held at most only a few hundred passengers and crew.
Apparently he had found and purchased what he wanted, very
likely of British (and Loyalist) origin, in New York, acquiring
the pieces, perhaps, as Christmas gifts for Martha.

A speed of eight knots in a favorable wind was "rattling
away." Sailing westward against the North Atlantic winds was
even more unpredictable, yet the shipment from the efficient
Lafayette to Washington arrived in Baltimore before the General could cancel it, with a bill for £129. Many pieces, to Washington's undisguised annoyance, duplicated his own purchases.

He arranged for their stowage with Jefferson in Annapolis, where Congress was still in session, until a wagon from Mount Vernon could retrieve the unwanted crates. Whatever his misgivings, he sent immediate payment to the Marquis, who was already, then, sailing to America to visit Washington, and would not see his reimbursement until much later.

Before another dinner at Cape's the next evening, December 2, where the enthusiasm was almost uninterrupted, there was, according to Lieutenant Colonel Benjamin Tallmadge, "a most splendid display of fire-works [which] far exceeded anything I had ever seen in my life." Shot above the bay from the Bowling Green, the illuminations were visible in the inner harbor, where some British vessels still lay. That may have been Washington's intention when, at West Point, he ordered the rockets and Roman candles "to celebrate the Peace" in New York, employing fireworks "which were intended to be exhibited at this post, or such of them as have not been injured by time, and can be transported."

Fireworks were often the hazardous responsibility of artillerymen. Rockets and flares, timed by the length of their fuses, were set upon scaffolding in a sequence to create patterns, or sent up by mortars or a short pipe with a lifting charge. Sometimes they were released individually by pyrotechnists, or in clusters, choreographed according to a "recipe" or formula, as a crank was turned to drive charged wheels, sometimes in opposite directions, to create designs on ignition via a miniature scratchboard, like a striking match. The chief ingredient was black powder, a ground mixture of potassium nitrate, sulfur, and charcoal, which created tails of amber colors when iron filings were added to the cylinders. When zinc powder was used, a greenish blue color was produced; saltpeter, sulfur, and antimony created a whitish color. Round "chrysanthemum" shells based on centuries-old Chinese technology would break open to fling out a thistlelike radial burst of stars.

Fired over the harbor beginning at six (it was nearly dark at five), one illumination, with thirty-four rockets, represented a dove descending with an olive branch of peace, which preceded a battery of rockets; another, employing twenty-eight rockets, took the shapes of two ships. A third, with forty-three rockets, showed Fame descending; and the display closed at seven with a mortar fusillade of one hundred fiery rockets. According to the *Pennsylvania Packet* and the *Salem Gazette*, the fireworks "infinitely exceeded every former exhibition in the United States; the prodigious concourse of spectators expressed their plaudits in loud and grateful clangors."

At eight that evening Judge Smith wrote to his wife from his refuge vantage on the *Ceres* that he "hope[d] to learn that no Accident happens by the Fireworks I see." Injuries from exploding or misdirected rockets were common. Afterward Washington asked Knox to thank the artillery officer, Captain William Price, and his assistants, who had arranged the "Fire-Works and Illuminations" originally intended to mark the departure from the garrison, "for the great skill and attention shewn in the conduct of that business."

Another thank-you message from Washington was to a feisty Dubliner, William Duke Moore, who sent the General, through the wife of a captain in the British Army's Volunteers of Ireland, now departing, a celebratory seal he had executed. Moore described it in an accompanying letter as "your Excellency in Front, Trampling on the late Enemy of your Country, pointing to a Ship Underway departing from the [American] Coast, with your Face at the same time turned to your Army, expressing the Motto by Virtue and Valour." It had taken nearly a year to reach him, as the letter was dated from Dublin on March 15, 1783 and

"Mrs. General Washington Bestowing Thirteen Stripes on Britannia," *Rambler Magazine* (London), March 1783.

H. A. Ogden's conception of the disbanding of the Continental Army in upstate New York is from *Harper's Weekly*, October 30, 1883.

Charles Willson Peale's portrait of Washington at the end of the war was reproduced in an engraving in *Harper's Weekly* on May 4, 1889, for the centenary of his inauguration as president.

ABOVE: Washington with Governor Clinton, both on horseback, leading troops into New York City is from an imaginative contemporary print.

BELOW: Howard Pyle's conception of the Continental Army marching into New York on November 24, 1783.

James Rivington holding a copy of his *Royal Gazette*. From a copy of the portrait by Gilbert Stuart.

John Van Arsdale hammering new cleats into the flagpole at Fort George, as imagined a century later in *Frank Leslie's Illustrated Newspaper* (New York), November 24, 1883.

ABOVE: Washington's farewell to his officers at Fraunces Tavern in the centenary drawing by Howard Pyle that appeared in *Harper's Weekly,* December 4, 1883.

BELOW: A nineteenth-century print of Fraunces Tavern at Pearl and Broad streets in New York, before its destruction by fire and modern restoration.

Henry Knox in a portrait by the book illustrator Alonzo Chappel. Knox's mutilated hand is discreetly placed and his girth de-emphasized.

The State House in Philadelphia, afterward Independence Hall, in a 1787 print from *Leslie's Magazine,* imagining how it looked a century earlier.

A reconstruction a century later by the architect Lester Hoadley Sellers, from contemporary descriptions, of Charles Willson Peale's Victory Arch on Market Street in Philadelphia. Scale is furnished by the onlookers standing at bottom left.

The State House in Annapolis, Maryland, where Washington resigned his commission on December 23, 1783, from a contemporary print.

Mann's Tavern in Annapolis, where Washington stayed for the resignation ceremony.

From a drawing by Polli Rodriguez in the Maryland State Archives.

ABOVE: John Trumbull in 1824 imagined the scene of Washington's resignation in the State House, Annapolis, including in the audience Martha Washington and her grandchildren (above right) and other women and children below who would not have been permitted on the floor. Copy from the original in the Capitol Rotunda, Washington, D.C.

BELOW: A contemporary print portraying Washington's resignation in Annapolis, perhaps accomplished earlier than Trumbull's canvas but slightly different in interior architecture and showing some men in the audience (possibly not Congressmen) standing and no women below.

Washington's study at Mount Vernon.

Martha Washington in an oval miniature painted by Charles Willson Peale in 1776 when he was serving as an officer with General Washington. Mrs. Washington was then forty-five.

Inset from John Trumbull's painting of Washington and his horse in New York with the harbor in the distance. From a study made in 1790 and completed in 1804, New York City Hall.

answered by the General on December 3, but the subject could not have been better timed. Washington praised Moore's "invention" and declared himself "extremely flattered by this mark of attention." Had the British authorities inspected it at any stage of its transit, the hostile work—the Irish had no love for their own occupiers—would never have reached the General.

Despite the concerns raised by Sir Guy, the recovery of New York had gone almost without a hitch. "The Civil Power," Washington informed Congress, also on December 3, "was immediately put in possession, and I have the happiness to assure you, that the most perfect regularity and good order have prevailed ever since. . . ." Like most of his hurried messages, it was dictated to and written by aides, often drafted entirely by them. The notes thanking Price and Moore and the message to Congress were in the hand of Lieutenant Colonel Benjamin Walker, once aide to, and interpreter for, military discipline impresario Baron Friedrich von Steuben, whose English was limited. He could swear only in German. Many other Washingtonian messages were written by Humphreys.

Finally, on Wednesday December 3, after a stormy sailing, the packet *Lord Hyde* arrived in New York with the treaty signed at Paris exactly three months earlier and then approved in London. The accord's opening language hardly seemed to concede British defeat and concessions and also implied American acceptance of High Anglican religious belief, but John Adams, Benjamin Franklin, and John Jay had apparently accepted the preamble as empty legalistic rhetoric necessary in formal British diplomacy. The French may have liked it much less, as it suggested that even Calais, the last English enclave in France, had not been retaken by the Duc de Guise in 1558. "In the Name of the Most Holy and Undivided Trinity," the treaty opened,

It having pleased the Divine Providence to dispose the hearts of the Most Serene and Most Potent Prince George the Third, by the Grace of God, King of Great Britain, France and Ireland, Defender of the Faith, Duke of Brunswick and Lünenburg, Arch Treasurer and Prince Elector of the Holy Roman Empire, &c., and of the United States of America, to forget all past misunderstandings and differences that have unhappily interrupted the good correspondence and friendship which they mutually wish to restore, and to establish such a beneficial and satisfactory intercourse between the two countries, and upon the ground of reciprocal advantages and mutual convenience, as may promote and secure to both perpetual peace and harmony. . . .

In Article I "His Britannic Majesty" recognized "the said United States" as "Free, Sovereign and Independent," listing the former colonies by name. "Beneficial" mutual relations were promised, but by the end of the month in which the treaty was approved, Parliament was continuing prohibitions on American trade. An "American Intercourse Bill" was shelved. The new nation, Edmund Burke complained, "had nothing to give in return." Exports from the sugar islands of the West Indies were to be made only in British bottoms, as a surplus of shipping loomed once all of Carleton's transports returned. In Rivington's *New York Gazette* on December 6, when the news reached the city, "Common Sense" (probably the once-notorious Thomas Paine, who was living bleakly on a small farm in New Rochelle) charged, "That a country has a right to be as foolish as it pleases, has been proved by the practice of England for many years past."

December y, 1783

6

FRAUNCES TAVERN

The General planned to start south on December 4, after the last of the congratulatory receptions and dinners that were crowding his days and the final flotilla under Sir Guy's command had embarked. That departure now seemed assured. One crucial (and very personal) farewell still loomed—to his remaining officers. Sentiment and increasing nostalgia tugged at Washington. Since he realized that he had to leave early enough that Thursday for some daylight traveling, he asked Sam Fraunces to prepare a noon luncheon in his elegant Long Room.

The last British vessels were scheduled to weigh anchor that morning, not only from relatively uninhabited Staten Island, but from Paulus Hook, Fort Tryon, Denyse's Ferry on the Brooklyn side of the Narrows at New Utrecht, and Laurel Hill. At various embarkation points overloaded redcoats abandoned twenty-two cannon, from puny six pounders to thirty-two pounders. Nearly isolated Paulus (Powles) Hook, a mile and a half across the Hudson from lower Manhattan, now part of Jersey City near Washington and Canal streets, was then a spit of sandy soil to which ferries sailed and other vessels could tie up. In August 1779 it had been the scene of an inconclusive raid ordered by Washington. Companies of Virginians and Marylanders under Major Henry Lee had attacked in the fog and withdrawn in confusion. Although the Marylanders took Hessian and British prisoners, the Virginians seeking the enemy earthworks lost their way crossing the protective salt marsh. It was now Washington's first homeward destination.

The *Pennsylvania Packet* reported that at Fraunces Tavern early on December 4, "the passions of human nature were never more tenderly agitated." (Rivington's *Gazette* reported much the same in its issue of December 6.) Realizing the inadequacy of a formal address at his leave-taking, Washington prepared none. Probably he could not trust his emotions to read one. Also, he had no idea how many of the officers who had entered the city with him, or were already there, would be present. The reception room was crowded when he entered at noon in his familiar blue and buff uniform. A "slight refreshment," as well as brandy and wine, awaited on the tables. Of the twenty-nine major generals commissioned by Congress during the war, only Knox, von Steuben, and McDougall were present. Most others had retired or resigned (or been discharged) since the war. Six had died, and one, who had arrived as a refugee in England on January 22, 1782, escaping after Yorktown, had betrayed Washington—Benedict Arnold.

Of the forty-four brigadier generals, only James Clinton, brother of the governor, was there, and one colonel of the line, Henry Jackson of Massachusetts. (Although promoted a grade in September, to remain on active duty he had become, on November 3, colonel of the downsized 1st American Regiment, the only remaining infantry regiment.) Happily not present was an irascible colonel breveted brigadier by the politics-ridden

Congress (to Washington's ire) only on September 30, when none were needed and officers were being released. While the terms of the peace treaty were being negotiated in Paris, the late-sixtyish, French-Irish Lewis Nicola, elderly at any rank, had written to Washington that the colonies ought to merge as a monarchy, with the already revered commander in chief as king. Washington replied strongly, "I must view [this suggestion] with abhorrence and reprehend [it] with severity."

Others had similar ideas but knew better than to push them on Washington. Six years later, in his will, Benjamin Franklin would write, "My fine crab-tree walking stick, with a gold head curiously wrought in the form of the cap of liberty, I give to my friend, and the friend of mankind, George Washington. If it were a sceptre, he has merited it and would become it." Franklin foresaw no throne in Washington's future, however, nor in the nation's. Earlier, in the shaky years of Confederation, Nicola saw a nation not topped by a crown as ripe for ruin. He was reacting to the weak, argumentative, and essentially headless Confederation government. Congress had a titular president who was not empowered to be an executive.

Washington recognized all the men of lesser ranks present at the tavern—lieutenant colonels, majors, and captains who had shared hardships with him. For him they were all authentic heroes, having remained in service, regardless of personal and family privation, to the end. If he kept his promise to himself to vanish into private life, he knew he would encounter few if any of them again.

Curiously, one apparently absent colonel, who had moved his law practice in November from Albany to New York City, slipping in ahead of the official reoccupation, was Washington's one-time aide-de-camp and former intimate, Alexander Hamilton. Banking on his credits in the General's service, he had written from Albany, where he was temporarily practicing law, late in September, asking to be retained nominally in the "peace establishment"—"without emoluments"—as an "honorary reward" for his wartime "sacrifice." Keeping his rank, he argued, would be "an agreeable circumstance" in his new "character," a bit of self-promotion for his practice. Hamilton had been in anxious correspondence with Washington about discontent in the army earlier in the year, offering suggestions for keeping "a *complaining* and *suffering* army within the bounds of moderation," and believed that his intrusions had been useful, but Washington now disappointed his former deputy. Explaining that Congress had left Princeton without establishing a peacetime army and also that consultation "with your particular friends" had been negative on grounds of the impropriety of making an exception, Washington tried to soften his rejection. Although he failed to close the letter with his usual "affectionately," in the final days of the Continental Army he promoted Hamilton via a brevet commission from lieutenant colonel to full colonel.

No thanks arrived from the petulant Hamilton, who lived and worked nearby at 56–57 Wall Street yet had made no documented effort to see Washington on his arrival in the city. Demonstrating his rancor by his absence, he was also not visible among the General's young men at Fraunces Tavern and would not be among the many who were invited warmly to visit after Christmas at Mount Vernon. The ambitious Hamilton, who wore his pride on his sleeve, would eventually renew his intimacy with Washington, which was mutually useful, but the break had been coming. Early in 1781, Hamilton had been eager to extricate himself from his role as Washington's administrative deputy, despite the power he wielded indirectly. He wanted to earn further fighting laurels before circumstances would make it too late. When thwarted, Hamilton had resigned from the commander in chief's staff.

Writing to his father-in-law, the rich and influential Hudson Valley baron Philip Schuyler, he claimed that in "the enthusiasm of the times" he had become "infected" with "an idea of the General's character which experience soon taught me to be unfounded," but it "overcame my scruples. For three years past I have felt no friendship for him and professed none." He promised that he would keep silent until the war was over, for Washington, he conceded, "was essential to the safety of America."

The General would relent with a belated field command, and Hamilton distinguished himself at Yorktown. Yet the rift lasted, despite superficial contacts, into 1786. When, in July 1787, Hamilton briefly left the Constitutional Convention in Philadelphia on personal business and then wrote to Washington while traveling, the General answered, "I am sorry you went away. I wish you were back." The words inferred much more.

At Fraunces Tavern the invitees milled about awaiting Washington's direction. He motioned to the men to help themselves from the buffet of cold meats but found himself emotionally unable to summon any appetite. He could hardly speak. Rather, he filled a goblet with wine and watched as others dutifully followed. Decanters were handed round the room in what was described by Lieutenant Colonel Tallmadge of the Second Continentals as "breathless silence." With glass raised, Washington waited until all had filled their own. "With a heart filled with love and gratitude," he began in a choked voice, "I now take leave of you. I most devoutly wish that your later days may be as prosperous and happy as your former ones have been glorious and honorable."

Overwrought, they mumbled confused responses to their chief's toast, swung their goblets about, and drank in some disorder to his health. Blinded by tears, his voice still faltering,

Washington resumed, "I cannot come to each of you, but shall feel obliged if each of you will come and take me by the hand." As the senior officer present, Henry Knox stepped forward silently and proffered his large cannoneer's fist. Weeping openly, Washington embraced his burly longtime chief of artillery and kissed him. (It was a time when the Anglo-Saxon stiff upper lip had not yet inhibited a display of manly emotions.) In turn, and by rank, each officer, von Steuben following, came forward to be clasped, "suffused with tears," and unable to utter an intelligible word.

"Such a scene of sorrow and weeping," Tallmadge recalled, "I had never before witnessed. . . . It was too affecting to be of long continuance—for tears of deep sensibility filled every eye—and the heart seemed so full, that it was wont to burst from its wonted abode. The simple thought that we were then about to part from the man who had conducted us through a long and bloody war, and under whose conduct the glory and independence of our country had been achieved, and that we should see his face no more in this world seemed to me utterly unsupportable." The General's parting band of brothers seemed like "grieving children." Each realized that they had all lived through something that would not be replicated in their lives, and that in the 1,600 mile length of the vast new nation, distance and time made it wholly impossible that they would share another such moment.

Once the most junior officer had received Washington's embrace, and men never known for tears were still dabbing at their eyes, he strode across the Long Room. With what seemed a strenuous effort, he raised his right arm in a silent farewell and walked out the door without looking back, passing through a waiting guard of light infantry and then along Pearl Street toward Whitehall and the Battery docks. Behind, not intending to overtake him and break the spell, most officers followed, Tallmadge remembered, "in mournful silence." Another observer

recalled the "mute and solemn procession, with dejected coun-
tenances, testifying feelings of delicious melancholy, which no
language can describe." No one would return for Samuel
Fraunces' carefully laid out collation of cold meats for which
Washington had paid the bill in advance.

It was two o'clock, late to begin a daylight journey in December. At the Whitehall wharf just to the east of Fort George, awaiting afternoon high tide, was Washington's already loaded barge,
again operated by Abraham Mesier's firm, although he had died
during the war, to ferry the General across the broad Hudson to
Paulus Hook, en route to Philadelphia and Annapolis. Ferries
were a varied lot, depending upon the depth and width of the
crossing and the strength of the current or the tides. Some required sail power; others were prodded across by barge poles or
propelled by oars; still others could be pulled across short distances on ropes tethered or flung to the opposite side. A contemporary engraving attributed to John Rogers shows Washington,
tricorn hat raised to the throngs on shore, crossing New York
harbor in a low-slung, beflagged boat powered by six oarsmen on
each side at the bow and five on each side at the stern.

Waiting to say goodbye were Governor Clinton and members
of the City Council. Also, according to Tallmadge, "a prodigious
crowd" had gathered. Accompanying the General down Whitehall
Street were a small dragoon guard, two servants, and his three
aides, David Humphreys, Benjamin Walker, and David Cobb. Von
Steuben would also travel with them as far as Philadelphia.

One wagon aboard contained whatever Washington had not
already sent home with Captain Howe and Christmas gifts he
wanted to bring to Mount Vernon himself. For Martha he already had lockets and sashes, hats and stockings, and an um-
brella. For his Custis step-grandchildren (Martha's son, Jack
Custis, had died of malaria at Yorktown in 1781), he had books,

a fiddle, and a whirlygig, a spinning toy sometimes with wind-mill-like sails. (Wooden motion toys were popular, weighted below to rock or spin—a sailing ship, a horse and rider, a row-boat with fisherman.) Nelly, four, and George Washington Parke Custis ("Wash"), two, became wards of the Washingtons when their mother remarried and took her elder two children with her, and the General once wrote of their pleasure in play-ing with their "Tea Sett, Grocer's Shop, Neat dress'd wax Baby, Smoking Man, books, and Box of Ginger br'd Toys." Also at Mount Vernon, soon, would be Martha's orphaned niece, Patty, and Washington's fatherless niece, Harriet, daughter of his brother Sam. The mortality rates made wards or adoptees of many whom Washington described as "little folks."

He also had collected some essentials for himself—more books, a new hunting rifle, bottles of wine, and such favorites as walnuts and brazil nuts, capers and olives, anchovies and raisins. Washington spent a great deal on wine, possibly because his perennially ill-fitting false teeth, made with hippopotamus ivory and metal, seemed always to pain him. (By 1789 he had only one natural tooth left and a set of wooden teeth.)

From Staten Island and Long Island farther out in the harbor, the last British transports were piping all hands aboard as Wash-ington's barge, with the General removing his hat and raising it in a visible farewell, pushed off. He had finally seen, he later wrote to James McHenry, "the backs of the British Forces turned upon us." Admiral Robert Digby would write to the Naval Office on January 8, 1784, after his flagship, Amphion, had made a fast passage into Portland harbor, "I left Staten Island the 5th Decem-ber, all the troops having sailed the day before. . . . Everything remained quite quiet when we came away."

At the dock, hats were lifted in return salute. Washington's old comrades remained bareheaded on the shore until the barge disappeared from view. It was a "scene so fraught with feeling," Tallmadge recalled, "that it seemed for a time as if it could never be erased from vivid and constant reflection." Yet as late as three generations after, some watchers imagined that Washington had "embarked on board the vessel which bore him to his home at Mount Vernon"—an unlikely voyage by barge.

Farther out at sea, as His Britannic Majesty's fifty-gun frigate *Assistance*, crowded with the cream of New York loyalists, was skirting Sandy Hook, the last spit of New Jersey land before the open Atlantic, six crewmen long planning to defect leaped from the ship into a waiting yawl manned by confederates and pressed toward the shore. Once an alarm was sounded aboard, a boat was lowered in pursuit, manned by a lieutenant and twelve seamen. When a sudden snow squall descended, they lost sight of the fleeing yawl and then of their own ship. The next morning, the bodies of all but one of them, including Lieutenant Hamilton Douglas Haliburton, brother of the Earl of Morton, washed up on a beach near what was then desolate Middleton Point. The missing sailor was never found. The six deserters disappeared.

Like Washington, Ben Tallmadge also had a home to revisit, at Brookhaven on Long Island. Absent for seven years, he returned in time for a spirited celebration on the village green at which his father (the local minister) and other happy villagers roasted an ox on a spit. "After a blessing from the God of Battles invoked by my father, I began to carve, dissect, and distribute [helpings] to the multitude around me. . . . A *Tory* could not have lived in that atmosphere one minute."

In W. M. Thackeray's novel *The Virginians* (1859), his sequel to *Henry Esmond* (1852), Colonel Esmond recalls, "with sometimes a break in his voice," his being at the already legendary adieu at Fraunces Tavern as his children and grandchil-

dren listen "touched and silent." In the American novelist
Weir Mitchell's once popular *Hugh Wynne: Free Quaker* (1896),
Wynne evokes in the last paragraphs of his fictional first-per-
son account his imagined presence as a young officer among
the "worn veterans of the winter camps and the summer bat-
tle-fields." Then he closes, "There is an old book my grandchildren love to hear me read to them. It is the *Morte d'Arthur,*
done into English by Sir Thomas Malory. Often when I read
therein of how Arthur the king bade farewell to the world and
to the last of the great company of his Knights of the Round
Table, this scene at Whitehall slip comes back to me, and I
seem to see once more these gallant soldiers, and far away the
tall figure of surely the knightliest gentleman our days have
known."

The press would recall Washington's "model," Lucius
Quinctius Cincinnatus, the fifth century B.C. Roman hero,
"who, victorious, left the tented field, covered with honor, and
withdrew from public life, to enjoy *civium cum dignitate.*" Recognizing Washington's similar intentions, his officers, Baron von
Steuben initiating the idea, had already formed a Society of the
Cincinnati. At the start, no one seemed to recall that as the
times became desperate, Cincinnatus was twice recalled from
his plow to become dictator.

Membership in the society was to be open to former officers
in the war and their eldest male descendants, with its objectives
to aid members and their families in cases of need and to promote the causes for which they fought. Some observers, nevertheless, had anxious second thoughts, that an hereditary order
might suggest a self-appointed aristocracy and even that it furnished, dangerously, a window of opportunity for a monarchy.
Soon popular opposition burgeoned as the Cincinnati was seen
as a threat to democratic institutions. Judge Aedanus Burke of

South Carolina published, in May 1784, an indictment hardly longer than its title, *Considerations on the Society or Order of Cincinnati: Lately Instituted by the Major-Generals, Brigadier-Generals, and other Officers of the American Army. Proving that it creates a Race of Hereditary Patricians, or Nobility. Interspersed with Remarks on its Consequences to the Freedom and Happiness of the Republic. Blow Ye the Trumpet in Zion.*

From France, Benjamin Franklin registered his disapproval by objecting wryly to the American bald eagle with outstretched wings as the society's symbol, since (as a bird of prey that often decapitated its live kills) it was "a bird of bad moral character." (Ever the diplomat, he accepted honorary membership.) John Adams, Sam Adams, and John Jay opposed it outspokenly. Although the clamor would fade, so would the Society of the Cincinnati, despite Washington's implied support in attending the initial meeting as its president with Knox as its secretary. In a few decades some state branches would wither away, but the Cincinnati, shorn of its threatening aspects, survived.

In a letter that would follow the General home, Richard Varick wrote from West Point on the day of Washington's departure from New York that his crew had finally "folded, sorted & properly endorsed & packed up in several Bundles" further papers, and three days later he added that the "lost papers are just come to Hand & I have folded but not had time to number them; they are in their respective Bundles. The Letter to me [with your instructions] was not open'd, but in perfect order & Muddy." By December 13 these also were on their way to Mount Vernon, to Washington's cluttered study on the ground floor, from which plantation business was overseen, and a tabletop screw-letterpress copied documents. A world diminished to that domestic sanctum was all he now wanted.

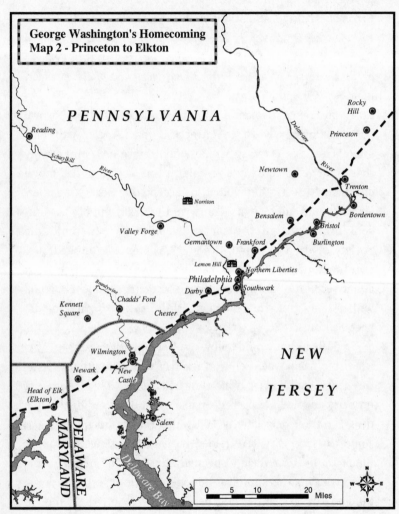

**George Washington's Homecoming
Map 2 - Princeton to Elkton**

PENNSYLVANIA

Reading

Schuylkill   River

Rocky
Hill

Princeton

Delaware   River

Newtown

Trenton

Norriton

Bensalem

Bordentown

Valley Forge

Bristol

Germantown   Frankford

Burlington

Lemon Hill

Philadelphia   Northern Liberties

Darby   Southwark

Brandywine

Chadds' Ford

Kennett
Square

Chester

NEW

Wilmington

Creek

Newark   New
Castle

JERSEY

Head of Elk
(Elkton)

DELAWARE

MARYLAND

Salem

Delaware Bay

0   5   10   20   Miles

N
W   E
S

Douglas Greenfield

7

TO PHILADELPHIA

With his Provost Guard in the lead, it took Washington four days, stopping at inns by evening, to traverse the hundred miles to Philadelphia, southward through New Brunswick and Trenton. Sometimes he switched from bouncing horseback to jolting carriage. He remembered the wintry routes through New Jersey well, scenes of small and rare triumphs that had kept alive the promise of independence, as when he had crossed the icy Delaware in wind, hail, and snow on Christmas night in 1776 to rout the surprised Hessians of Colonel Johann Rall at Trenton. Contemptuously, the alcoholic Rall had referred earlier to the ragged and freezing army across the river as "country clowns." Of the 1,200 Hessians (in all but a few engagements, like Saratoga and Yorktown, the numbers on both sides, by later standards, were small), 106 were killed or wounded and 912 taken prisoner. Only four Americans died, two from frostbite. They were probably shoeless.

In contrast now, New Jersey villages and towns appeared merry, with flags, bunting, bands, and banners. Much of New

Jersey under its vanished royal governor, Benjamin Franklin's illegitimate son William,* had been openly Loyalist. Once in bleak 1776 when Washington had urged Jerseymen to join him, only thirty in the village of Newark came forward, but three hundred the same day volunteered under the Union Jack. Retreating southward through the colony with the remnants of his army, Washington had called upon local farmers and villagers to scorch the earth before the enemy; instead they welcomed the British as bearers of peace. Even when New Jerseyites joined his own side and he asked them to swear allegiance to the United States, they stubbornly refused, declaring, "New Jersey is our country!" Now, elated residents cheered as Washington's cavalcade clattered by, and local councillors stepped forward waving sheets of laudatory addresses. Each such salute required a stop for a courteous reply, and David Humphreys and the other aides scratched out brief responses on which Washington could improvise.

"Festive crowds impeded his passage through all the populous towns," Humphreys recalled floridly; "the devotion of a whole people pursued him with prayers to Heaven for blessings on his head, while their gratitude sought the most expressive language of manifesting itself to him, as their common father and benefactor." (Washington would read the ornate passage in Humphreys' draft biography and approve it.)

Very likely Washington's route through Elizabeth, New Brunswick, and Trenton, the later U.S. Route 1, was a carriage road that followed an old Indian trail. Indian scouts had known

---

*William Franklin had been arrested by the rebel Provincial Congress of New Jersey and imprisoned at East Windsor, Connecticut. Returned to New York in October 1778 after being exchanged for the "president" (governor) of Delaware, John McKinley, held by the British, he remained in the city until it was clear it would be returned to the Americans. In August 1782 he sailed for England.

the easiest paths with the fewest natural obstacles. At the end of October, Elias Boudinot had completed his year as president of Congress and escaped forthwith to Elizabeth and his law practice, but there is no evidence that he saw Washington pass. Retreating into privacy, he would write only that he, too, was "again enjoying the sweets of Domestic Life on my little Estate here rescued from the Hands of a Powerful Enemy after a seven year explulsion," but esteemed it "one of the greatest Honors of my life" that he had served his country "in Conjunction with & under the Direction of Genl Washington."

At New Brunswick, once called Inian's Ferry but renamed for George I, who was also Duke of Brunswick, Washington stood in his halted carriage to declare his hope that citizens would esteem "those Worthy and deserving Men who have so eminently contributed to the glorious termination of the War." The town held happier memories for him than many other wartime sites. Although he had retreated there from New York in 1776 and then had to evacuate it on the approach of General Howe, he returned after the Battle of Monmouth in 1778. It was from New Brunswick in mid-1781 that he issued orders for the final march south to Yorktown. "Although I am now returning to a much wished for retirement," he closed, "yet I cannot bid adieu to the acquaintances and connections I have formed while acting in a public character without experiencing a certain pleasing, melancholy sensation, pleasing because I leave my country in the full possession of liberty and independence, melancholy because I bid my friends a long, perhaps a last farewell."

After his previous visit to the area, to attend commencement exercises at the College of New Jersey, its board of trustees had voted to commission Charles Willson Peale of Philadelphia to paint the General's portrait, to replace "the picture of the late king of Great-Britain"—George III's grandfather, George II—"which was torn away by a [six-pound] ball from the American artillery in the battle of Princeton." Washington had created the vacant space at Nassau Hall for his own likeness.

This time, he bypassed Princeton and went on to nearby Trenton, the state capital, where he addressed the legislature on the afternoon of December 6, a Saturday. Again his most wooden phrases were the product of the prolific pen of the busy Humphreys. Washington was introduced in the General Assembly by Governor William Livingston, as he knew he would be, by allusions to the amazing Christmas night 1776 skirmishes with the Hessians, which had already receded into myth. (Fortunately, the Hessians were less than watchful in the aftermath of their traditional German Christmas carousing.) To the governor the achievement was "Your signal victory over an enemy till then, through the great superiority of their numbers, the triumphant possessors of this part of the country." In Humphreys' turgid draft, Washington replied, "I cannot however suppress the effusions of my gratitude for their flattering allusion to an event which hath immortalized the name of Trenton. . . ." Above "immortalized," which Washington crossed out, he substituted "signalized." It was no improvement.

In a phrase Washington would employ often on the journey home, he spoke of bidding his audience "a long farewell." It was also an exhausting one. He would rise to deliver an exhortation wherever a small crowd gathered at a crossroads or marketplace or village common. With little or no idea of local history he would commend listeners as having been stubborn patriots. All he knew is that they had not fled as many Loyalists had done. They were there. Sometimes he recommended his audiences "to the indulgent care of Heaven." And, as he often did in addressing official bodies, he declared, in an utopian entreaty, "May unanimity and wisdom ever prevail in your public councils! May Justice and liberality distinguish the Administration of your Government!"

Few in his outdoors audiences could have realized how grueling Washington's pilgrimage home was. Roads were narrow, muddy, and cratered. Horses had to be fed, watered, and rested. So, too, servants, soldiers, and companions. Darkness and chill came early in December, and Washington's aides had to procure places for the party to sleep, from an inn for the General to barns and straw pallets for those in the lowest ranks. Greeted at almost every village, Washington had to appear dignified, however weary he felt. Much as he savored the relentless welcomes, he longed for an ending to the triumphal progress. Yet the impromptu human telegraph of excited citizens on horseback would spread the word about where he was, or would soon be, at almost every milepost he passed. Large crowds and small groups kept gathering to catch a glimpse of the soul of the revolution.

The narrowest passage across the Delaware below Trenton was Blazing Star Ferry. On December 8, barges conveyed the General's carriages and horses to Pennsylvania. Late that Monday afternoon, as twilight approached, he reached the village of Frankford, north of Philadelphia. A stone barn there, along Frankford Creek, near Swede's Mill, stored army ordnance and muskets. An official greeting party awaited. John Dickinson, who chaired the state's Executive Council, held the highest rank. Robert Morris, also there, was still the army's irreplaceable financier. Present, too, was former major general Arthur St. Clair, who in 1777 had prudently abandoned Fort Ticonderoga without a fight—a court martial cleared him—and had helped settle the mutiny of the Pennsylvania line (which had impelled the shabby flight of Congress to Princeton). In the final days of the war he was with Washington at Yorktown. Edward Hand, former Adjutant General of the Continentals, once a lowly surgeon's mate in an Irish regiment, had just returned to his medical practice in Philadelphia. Other local dignitaries accompanied them—loyal Germans from Germantown, then an independent entity, and black-garbed Quakers from the city itself.

The elite City Troop of Light Horse, in smart red and blue uniforms, met them as escorts. Clattering southward toward Philadelphia, often within sight of the broadening Delaware, they passed along miles of woods and farms, finally reaching, in darkness, the characteristic redbrick buildings and cobblestone inner streets. With more than forty thousand inhabitants, Philadelphia was the size of Boston and New York combined. It seemed that the entire population of the Quaker City milled about in the dusty torchlit streets to salute Washington, opening a path as he approached. Church bells rang; cannon boomed; a Dutch ship in the harbor fired the familiar thirteen rounds.

In the heady atmosphere, a Philadelphia weekly, in labored verses "On Peace," had already celebrated the commander in chief in lines that suggested that the sometimes despondent Washington, unsure he could hold his army together, had never been disheartened. "On Delaware's majestic tide," the poet declared, the "lillies" of peace floated, and "disbanding armies quit the plain," while "thund'ring navies leave the main." Since gratitude was owed not only to the "Great Ruler of the skies," but to the Deity's designated general,

Let WASHINGTON'S immortal name,

Loudly swell the trump of fame;
That gallant Chief, long press'd with care,
Whose bosom never knew despair!
Him shall the just historian's pen
Shortly proclaim the First of Men:
His wond'rous deeds the muse engage
And deathless live from age to age!

Another "Ode to Peace" had included the worshipful line, "While earth exists, great Washington will live!" In a similar tone, the editor of the *Pennsylvania Journal* had already written, extravagantly, "All panegyrick is vain and language too feeble to express our ideas of his greatness. May the crown of glory he has placed on the brow of the genius of America, shine with untarnished radiance and lustre, and in the brightness of its rays be distinctly seen—WASHINGTON, THE SAVIOUR OF HIS COUNTRY!" Caught in that national mood, he had every reason to believe that the only way he could forestall further lionization was to extricate himself from both public duty and public visibility.

With his aides, the General was escorted to the fashionable City Tavern, on Second Street above Walnut, which had opened in 1773 and was known for its elegant, wainscoted interior and its baked oysters and Madeira. Washington had dined there before, and it had been patronized by the fastidious (and indolent) General William Howe and his staff during the occupation. Joseph Stansbury, a British agent in Philadelphia in 1777, had described Howe disapprovingly as a "Carpet Knight," more active in taverns, ballrooms, and bedrooms than on the field of battle. A year before the Declaration of Independence he had been embarrassed in Massachusetts at Bunker Hill (actually adjacent Breed's Hill) and ever after preferred to limit his frontal assaults to the fairer sex. He had no stomach for what he saw as an impossible war. Since the colonists might not be enthusiastic for union, but wanted Britain even less, Howe had even recommended to Whitehall before the Declaration was voted upon in the early summer of 1776 that it might be best "to withdraw completely . . . and leave the colonists to war with each other."

Washington was put up in Morris's mansion—not the first such honor for the financier, and an expense off the books. Morris owned two dwellings in the city. His house on Front Street below Dock Street, adjacent to rooms where he once had his Office of Finance, was not splendid enough to lodge the General. Morris was also squire of "The Hills," a spacious stone dwelling on a knoll now called Lemon Hill, on the eastern bank of the Schuylkill (Dutch for hidden creek). Three miles from Morris's town house, the rolling slopes of the farm stretched south from the present Girard Avenue to Fairmont, where a waterworks would be built on the southwestern five acres of the estate. Cattle grazed on the greensward and sheep browsed; oranges, lemons, and pineapples flourished in Morris's hothouses. John Jay, Alexander Hamilton, Generals Greene and Gates, and Lafayette had all been guests during the war, as had Washington, and the General and his servants and aides received renewed hospitality according to rank, as a gardener's house and two farmhouses on the property furnished accommodation. Except for the months of Howe's occupation of Philadelphia, when Morris's family fled, with their most prized possessions, in a procession of covered wagons to the town of Manheim, northwest of Lancaster, the financier flourished at The Hills.

One servant apparently with Washington from the beginning ("all the War"), but for his capture by the British and release in 1776 (prisoner exchanges were then common), was an outsized mulatto slave, William Lee, called Billy. In July 1784, when Washington would attempt to retrieve Margaret Thomas, to whom Billy was "attached," he described Lee to Clement Biddle of Philadelphia as someone who "has lived with me so long and followed my fortunes through the War with fidility." Free, or freed, Margaret Thomas was someone about whom Washington wrote to Biddle, "I never wished to see her more yet I cannot refuse his request." Separated by war from Billy Lee, she lived in Philadelphia with a free black couple, Isaac and Hannah Sills, who cooked for local families.

Slaves were usually invisible (it was a common pretense), but at least one—the loyal William Lee—not only served Washington throughout the revolution but quietly returned with him to Mount Vernon. Israel Trask, who volunteered for the Massachusetts line in 1775, when he was only ten, accompanying his father, a lieutenant, seventy years later, in 1845, remembered Washington and Billy together early in the war. Perhaps distance in time added to the drama. "I only saw him and his colored servant, both mounted. With the spring of a deer, he leaped from his saddle, threw the reins of his bridle into the hand of his servant, and rushed into the thickest of the melee, [and] with an iron grip seized two tall, brawny, athletic, savage-looking riflemen by the throat, keeping them at arm's length, alternately shaking and talking to them. In this position the eye[s] of the belligerent[s] caught sight of the general. Its effect on them was [their] instantaneous flight at the top of their speed. . . . Less than fifteen minutes time had elapsed from the commencement of the row before the general and his two criminals were the only occupants of the field of action." Much bloodshed, Trask thought, had been prevented, "by the physical and mental energies timely exerted by one individual." The two enemy prisoners were led away, and Billy Lee returned the reins to Washington. It had been one of the rare occasions when the General's devoted slave was even noticed at his side. Lee could have defected easily when briefly a prisoner of war. He did not, and remained with Washington all his life.

"Much engaged with General Washington," Morris noted briefly in his diary on December 9, a Tuesday. His office at Fifth and Market (formerly High) streets had been the destination of the five hundred soldiers barracked in Northern Liberties who had marched down Fourth Street earlier in the year to demand their pay. Washington spent part of nearly every day that week settling his own accounts, seeing little of the wartime neglect in drab outlying streets, where broken windows remained unrepaired, paint peeled from door frames, missing cobblestones in the streets were unreplaced, and buildings that had housed soldiers and horses still reeked.

Misfortune seemed absent from the city center, where redbrick buildings reposed behind walled gardens and tall oaks loomed over streets stirring with commerce. Wharves on the Delaware were loaded with merchandise. Local newspapers boasted of increasing trade and normalization. Margaret Trotter advertised "choice" pickles, mangoes, walnuts, cucumbers, beans, ketchup, vinegar, and "pockmilions" at her shop in Elfreth's Alley, some of her produce from the West Indies. George Hughes, from his store on Market Street "next the wharff," purveyed "Pipes, Hogsheads and Quarter Casks, old Madeira Wine; Lisbon Wines, of the vintage of 1779, in Quarter Casks; old Cane juice Spirits, West Indian Rum, French Brandy; excellent Hyson and Souchong Teas in Quarter Chests; Pepper by the Bale, Mace, Cinnamon, Nutmegs, Cloves, Coffee . . . and a few H[ogs]h[ea]ds choice Muscovado sugars." For Philadelphians doing repair or construction, he also had window glass and "white lead."

Francis Knox, master of the *Congress,* announced his ship's sailing to Londonderry "in a short time" and still had "exceeding good Accommodations" for passengers and space for more cargo. He boasted of "the swiftness of this Ship's sailing." James Gregory's brewery at Fourth and Race streets offered beer and porter to "Merchants and Captains of Ships" and delivery of pale ale and "table beer" to "private Families and public Houses, on the shortest Notice, by a Line or verbal Message." Daniel Goodman, from Arch Street between Second and Third, offered not only kegs of "small Biscuit" but his family's "Old England" easy and infallible cure of "the Bite of a Mad Dog."

The normalization was not at all normal by modern standards. The practice of indentured service continued. Richard Gibbs of suburban Bensalem offered ten years' time of "a stout, healthy Mulattoe Girl" of sixteen. Isaac Hilbert of Darby offered an eight dollar reward for the seizure of a florid, round-faced Irish servant of nineteen, William McNeely, last seen wearing a sailor jacket, red waistcoat, blue breeches, and "an old castor Hat," who had run away; and John Dunlap of Philadelphia offered five pounds' reward for the return of an obviously eye-catching servant girl of twenty-one from Belfast, Jenny Stevenson, with "blue eyes and black hair, a tall, lusty, hearty fresh-looking wench" wearing "two striped lincey* petticoats, a striped red calicoe short gown, and a black Barcelona handkerchief." Masters of vessels were reminded of the unrepealed British laws forbidding the harboring of runaways. The land it-

---

*Linsey-woolsey was a coarse sturdy fabric of wool and linen or cotton.

self was wide, however, and the frontier westward beyond Philadelphia seemingly endless.

On the afternoon of the ninth an address of homage to Washington was laid before the Supreme Executive Council of Pennsylvania by John Dickinson, in effect the governor and his cabinet, expressing "sincere joy" on the General's "return in safety and health to this city," and congratulating him "heartily" on the "honorable peace." He was thanked for his "love of your fellow-citizens," who ardently wished for him "every happiness of this life" and beseeched "the best and greatest of Beings, in his good time, to bestow upon you the felicities of that to come." Three days later a response from Washington was read, thanking them for his "welcome reception" and reciprocating "all your benevolent wishes."

The General spoke to the General Assembly of Pennsylvania, with the busy Humphreys penning stylistic changes on Washington's familiar themes. The redbrick, white-steepled State House, built in 1748 at Sixth and Chestnut streets, two blocks from Morris's office and close to the western edge of the expanding city (few dwellings existed beyond Eighth Street), had been the meeting place of the Continental Congress in 1775 when it appointed Washington as general and again in 1776 when it adopted the Declaration of Independence. On July 2, 1776, it had approved a resolution, first moved on June 7, "that these United Colonies are, and of right ought to be, free and independent States." Three days later—July 5—the Congress had a revised text printed and dated July 4, but delegates did not sign a definitive document embodying the bill until August 2, 1776. Inevitably the building would lose its identity as State House and become Independence Hall, and to the surprise of many, July 4 would become a formal Independence Day because Thomas Jefferson had insisted that the acceptance rather than the signing was what counted.

At the State House, George Gray, the Speaker of the General Assembly, praised the "inestimable legacy" Washington had "bequeathed" to America, as well as the General's desire to step aside "when your sword was no longer necessary for our defence." And Gray closed hopefully, "May your Excellency be long spared to this country; and among the sweets of domestic life, may you have the happiness of beholding a growing empire, wise, just and united."

"I consider the approbation of the Representatives of a free and virtuous People," Washington responded, "as the most enviable reward that can ever be conferred on a public Character." Although the Pennsylvania legislature, like the other twelve, was often difficult and quarrelsome in responding to requests from Congress for funds, provisions, and troops, he diplomatically glossed over past frustrations in his "final farewell," acknowledging instead "the assistance I have frequently derived from your State. . . ." Again he closed with the utopian benediction, "May the Representatives and Citizens of this Commonwealth continue to possess the same good dispositions, and may they be as happy in the enjoyment of Peace as it is possible for a wise, just, and united People to be."

Recognizing that national unity was in danger of eroding as wartime national purpose diminished, Washington, always emphasizing the positive, was making his journey home for Christmas a campaign for cohesiveness as a nation. However, he remained adamant about retirement. Reviewing his likely schedule he wrote to Congressman McHenry, "On Monday next I expect to leave the City, and by slow travelling arrive at Baltimore on Wednesday, where I will spend one day and then proceed to Annapolis and get translated into a private citizen."

One of the many problems fracturing the papered-over unity of the states was that they were reluctant to abrogate wartime laws conflicting with the peace terms. On the next day, December 10, 1783, a member of Congress wrote to a Virginia legislator, "I am, myself, *principled against* [loyalist] refugees and British debts. I think the former will make wretched Republicans, and to the latter, in my opinion, all just title has been forfeited. But let us see what the faith of America as a nation, and her interests as a people, require, and leaving all prejudice against those people aside, act in conformity thereto. Our conduct, or rather the conduct of some very wild and unthinking people scattered throughout the United States, has hurt us much in the eyes of all Europe." It was harmful, he contended, to be "humiliating to Great Britain."

The brilliant young Hamilton, twenty-six, who was already having it both ways by acting as patriot attorney representing royalist claimants, would, like the conciliatory congressman, admonish those Americans who approved a solemn and valid treaty of peace and then cited state laws to evade paying for it, or abiding by it. They reminded him of the unprincipled Roman general who, having promised Antiochus III to restore half his vessels, sawed them in two before returning half of each ship, and also of the unscrupulous Plataeans, who, having agreed to release prisoners of war, murdered them and returned them dead. States that were already flouting their war-born union were in danger of fragmenting it, as Sir Guy Carleton, now no longer a player, had been predicting hopefully.

Such dire possibilities were left unspoken as Washington collected honors in Philadelphia, where Philip Freneau wrote of the General in verses dated the tenth,

> *Thy worth disdains all vulgar fame*
> *Transcends the noblest poet's praise. . . .*

While civic bodies and delegations in Philadelphia vied to compliment the General, perhaps the greatest tribute came indirectly that December 10 when local portraitist Charles Willson Peale, who would do eight portraits of Washington from life, one begun that day, wrote about him to expatriate Philadelphia artist Benjamin West. The official history painter to George III and by implication a royalist, West had been asked to help sell in England a full-length portrait of Washington, which Peale would ship across the Atlantic. West responded helpfully, adding that it would be "a great delight" to see, if only on canvas, "that greatest of all characters, *General Washington*, . . . that phinominy among men." He added his congratulations to Peale "and my countrymen in general, on the event of the Peace and the fortitude they have shown during the unhappy war. Their wisdom and unshaken perseverance enroll them forever among the greatest charactors of antiquity."

Discussing pictures with the King, and frankly confessing his ambition to paint Washington, West was asked what he thought the General would do when peace finally came. Would he remain in command of the army? Would he become head of state? He could be anything he wanted to be. West said that he had learned that Washington wanted only to return to his farm.

The King was astonished. If Washington does that, His Majesty declared, he will be the greatest man in the world.

West himself wanted to paint "a set of pictures containing the great events which have affected the revolution of America," and by letter Peale suggested, among the possibilities, Washington's "The Taking of the Hessians at Trent Town." He added that General Joseph Reed (an officer whose criticism of Washington early in the war had not short-circuited their friendship) was carrying Peale's portraits of both Washington and Nathanael Greene to London—as was now possible—to have plates engraved. "Your advice would oblige me."

The General's Thursday in Philadelphia remained free of appointments. Recommended by Congress, December 11 had been proclaimed a day of "Public Thanksgiving." The nation's first official Thanksgiving Day, celebrated, as future observances would be, on a Thursday, had actually come earlier. In a proclamation issued in Poughkeepsie on November 16, before setting off southward, Washington had declared that Thursday as a "Day of Public Thanksgiving, for the final establishment of American Independence, and the long desired restoration of Civil Government, in the blessings of an Honourable Peace."At the Brick Meeting House in Beekman Street in New York, reopened for the event, Presbyterian minister Dr. John Rodgers, who had been an army chaplain, gave a sermon using as a text a verse from Psalm 126: " The Lord hath done great things for us; whereof we are glad." Recognizing, nevertheless, the many Loyalists in the pews, he added the perfunctory and traditional prayer for King George, and young Peter Augustus Jay, John Jay's son, nearly seven, living then with his grandparents in New Jersey while his father was in France, shook his head in visible objection.

In Philadelphia, even Morris's busy finance office was shut. Washington may have utilized part of the holiday to explore shops for additional Christmas gifts, as Philadelphia was the mercantile hub of the former colonies and he expected that Martha's daughter-in-law, Nelly, and her four small children, Washington's step-grandchildren, would all be waiting at Mount Vernon.

Washington had often patronized the merchant and broker Clement Biddle, who, from 38–45 Walnut Street, near the Delaware docks, purveyed everything from barrels of coffee beans to silver tableware and fine lace. One of the "fighting Biddles" of brothers and cousins despite their Quaker heritage, Clement Biddle had left his business to help organize the "Quaker Blues." He fought at Trenton, Brandywine, Germantown, and Monmouth, and then became deputy quartermaster general with the rank of colonel. Nicholas Biddle had been killed at sea in 1778 while commanding the *Randolph*, overmatched against the British two-decker *Yarmouth*, and Charles Biddle joined the Quaker Light Infantry, then moved on to command fighting ships, twice becoming a prisoner of war. Again in his civilian role, Clement Biddle did not supply everything, but he could find, and forward, almost anything Washington wanted.

For himself, in Philadelphia, Washington acquired a spare pair of spectacles. David Rittenhouse, the greatest American astronomer, who had made observations on the transit of Venus from his farm at Norriton, above the Schuylkill, in 1769, finding that the planet had an atmosphere, ground the lenses. At his city home at 7th and Mulberry Streets, Rittenhouse also repaired a misaligned theodolite—a surveyor's instrument for measuring angles—which Washington had sent him earlier.

The General had made good use of his original eyeglasses. "The Spectacles suit my Eyes extremely well, as I am persuaded the reading glasses also will when I get more accustomed to the use of them," he had written in thanking Rittenhouse, who would accept no payment for either pair. "At present I find some difficulty in coming at the proper Focus; but when I do obtain it, they magnify properly and show objects very distinctly which at first appear like a mist blended together and confused."

When yet another mutiny had threatened over lack of pay, at Newburgh in March, his earlier set of spectacles had proved strategically useful, as the General staged a personal appeal. An anonymous "fellow officer" (possibly Major John Armstrong, Jr., son of a major general) had circulated a manifesto arguing that officers about to be mustered out should not lay down their arms until their ungrateful country had paid them their due. Privately, he had described the ranks as "loud and insolent," officers as "broken, dissatisfied and desponding," and Congress as "weak as water and impotent as old age." Before a mass meeting could be held to air the desperate discontent, the General had called all officers to one of his own in The Temple, a wooden structure used for religious and social occasions.

Despite unconcealed grumbling, they had packed the hall, where Washington urged them to "place a full confidence in the purity of intentions of Congress." He hardly believed what he was saying himself, hoping aloud that posterity would be able to record that "the glorious example you have exhibited" was "the last stage of perfection to which human nature was capable of attaining." To validate the sincerity of Congress he pulled from a pocket a letter from Joseph Jones, in which the Virginia congressman prayed that the army "would exercise awhile longer, at least, that patient forbearance, which hath hitherto so honourably distinguished them." Stumbling over the sentences, Washington was forced to affix his new reading glasses. "Gentlemen, you must pardon me," he said humbly, "I have grown grey in your service and now find myself growing blind."

If melodrama can be subtle, he had accomplished that paradox. His listeners were stunned. Word of his gesture spread, and accommodation followed. But resolution also required Morris's importing kegs of silver half-crowns and *livres*, displayed with the barrel tops theatrically knocked off so that Continentals could see the promised hard cash.

Not only foot soldiers and their officers remained unpaid. Embittered, Captain John Paul Jones had appealed to Morris on

October 13, 1783, "Permit me to call the attention of Congress to the Interest of the gallant Officers and brave Men who served in the Squadron I had the Honor to command. . . . It is now four Years since the Services which were performed which did so much Honor to themselves and to the Flag of America, yet they have not in all that Time received any gratification either in respect of Wages, Bounties, Prize money, or [for] the losses which many of them sustained when the *Bonhomme Richard* sunk. . . ." No compensation came.

Closeted with Morris, Washington still worked on the reimbursement of his own remaining accounts. Early in October he had asked for $4,000, of which $2,500 was to cover the closing outlays for himself and his party, and a further $1,500 for the wartime travels of Mrs. Washington, on her way home from Rocky Hill after a last visit to him, settled so "that she should procure at Philadelphia some Articles of Furniture, and Stores for my House in Virginia." Philip Audibert, Paymaster General John Pierce's assistant in Philadelphia, had found the funds, and very likely the resourceful Clement Biddle arranged for her needs.

Washington had interpreted his insistence upon serving without pay but with his expenses to be reimbursed to include, broadly, the cost of all equipment, travel, official entertainment, and any personal necessities (like Martha, on occasion) he required while living away from home. When Humphreys later wanted to write an account of Washington's life, the General cautioned that, to avoid misunderstanding, it might be "necessary to mention that my time & Services were given to the public without compensation, and that every direct and indirect attempt afterwards, to reward them (as appeared by . . . the vote of 50 shares in each of the Navigations of Potomack & James River by the State of Virginia who knew that I would refuse anything that should carry with it the appearance of reward . . .). But he has constantly declined accepting of any compensation . . . , or provision for the augmented expenses which have been incurred in consequence of his public employment. . . ."

Washington never explained what the "augmented expenses" he incurred were—perhaps Rivington's golden guineas paid over in New York were included. He listed for Morris all gratuities he had laid out, unidentified costs confidentially incurred out of his pockets in behalf of his Secret Service, and those accounted for in a ledger in which he had personally, if sometimes vaguely, itemized expenses verified by vouchers from his aides. On the same day that John Paul Jones had entreated Morris, he noted in his diary, "Colo[nel Mathias] Ogden called respecting a Claim he has for Money for secret Service &s. I referred him to the General for Settlement thereof." Spies and informants did not come cheap. Morris would reimburse Washington for such outlays without naming names, and the General, as with Rivington, would have to settle them himself.

A letter quoted in the *Pennsylvania Gazette* after Washington returned to Virginia reported that while in Philadelphia, he delivered his complete accounts to the Comptroller, for Morris, "in a book. It comprehends a period of 8 years *all in his own hand writing*—and every entry made in a most particular manner, stating the occasion of each charge, so as to give as little trouble as possible in examining them. In this you see he has been as exemplary as in every other part of his conduct. Happy it would be for the United States, had each person who has handled public money been equally exact and punctual!" Even then, little could be kept from the press.

The document still exists, with a final total in dollars of $64,335.30. All expense entries are listed, in "The United

States in Account with G. Washington," in "lawful money" in dollars or at six shillings in the colonial pound, with their equivalent in dollars. Partial payments had been made as recently as July 1, 1783, but all were incomplete, and to them Washington now supplemented accountings of Martha's visits to his various headquarters, including her travel costs, since 1775. Although these seemingly domestic matters might have been covered from his own private purse, over his signature he itemized them as totaling £1,064, and "lawful." They were duly accepted as proper charges by James Milligan, then Comptroller of the Treasury, to whom Washington returned $27,770 in rather useless Continental paper money as unexpended from his military chest.

Drawing a new warrant for £217.16.8 on his accounts due, Washington found later that he was being paid at the devalued rate of Pennsylvania currency and had to await still further settlements that were unequal in depreciated paper to his actual outlays. At home he would have no cash to spare, and the roof leaked.

On the same day, the busy thirteenth, Timothy Pickering, the Quartermaster General, filed with Morris his outlays for the reoccupation of New York, including forage for horses, which cost two thousand dollars, twice what he had originally estimated. He also had to pay discharged officers and the costs of transporting their baggage home, and for three hundred cords of wood, presumably for official fires. Morris issued him a warrant for five thousand dollars, which he was able to do, among other kiting transactions to buy time, by overdrawing the 1782 Dutch loan.

When Washington left Philadelphia he had yet to file his expenses while in the city and would have more costs to report by the time he surrendered his commission at Annapolis. One outlay involved David Cobb, whom he authorized to leave for home on account "of domestic and other concerns." Washington allocated Cobb a hundred dollars for his travel expenses. Over their protests, the General would give his other aides-de-camp, Walker and Humphreys, equivalent funds, itemized later as the final entry in his accounts, three days after Christmas. As he would explain to the Comptroller, "Their finances I well knew were unable to bear it, altho I had some difficulty to prevail on them to accept this aid." Yet their active duty pay, they knew, would end effective with his resignation. (Among other expenses in Philadelphia he would list were $49.05 for "sundry" payments made for him by Colonel Cobb and $7.40 for eight days of "waiters" and "washing." He seemed to leave nothing out. It was his due.)

Unable to talk business with Washington as he bypassed Princeton, the Reverend John Witherspoon had followed the General to Philadelphia. A Scottish-born Presbyterian minister who was also president of the College of New Jersey, Witherspoon had been a tireless patriot during the war, a member of the Continental Congress from 1776 through 1782, and on its board of war as well as the committee for secret correspondence on foreign affairs. He was also an ambitious entrepreneur for his religious flock (and himself) and wanted to discuss what Washington called "my Lands to the westward of the Allighaney mountains," how much acreage the General owned, and "the terms upon which I would lease them." He had, Washington would explain, patents signed by the former royal governor of Virginia, Lord Dunmore, "for about 30,000 acres; and Surveys for about 10,000 more," but transfer had been "suspended by the disputes with Gr. Britain." (At the time Virginia unrealistically claimed vast territories reaching at least to the Mississippi.) The land grants had been made in 1763, at the conclusion of the frontier wars with the French, to reward serving officers, as was Washington, "according to his rank, and to the private Soldier, certain quantities."

Some of Washington's lands ("Washington's bottom") stretched along the south shore of the Ohio River near what is now Wheeling; below, further acreage bordered on the banks of the "Great Kanawha," which he described as "a river nearly as large, and quite as easy in its navigation." As a young surveyor he had explored the area and described "the whole of it" as "rich bottom land, beautifully situated . . . and abounding plentiously in Fish, wild fowl, and Game of all kinds." He was willing to rent portions on long- or short-term leases, as he wanted to make up his wartime losses in income, but "I cannot think of separating for ever from Lands which are . . . abundantly blessed with many natural advantages."

Since Witherspoon wanted to settle flocks of Presbyterians on the frontier, Washington assured him that "it would give me pleasure to see these Lands seated by particular Societies, or religious Sectaries with their Pastors. It would be a means of . . . making life, in a new and rising Empire. . . ."

Although Witherspoon would encourage the settlement of immigrant Scots-Irish on the frontier, he would remain in New Jersey, later, at sixty-eight, marrying a widow of twenty-four. Prudently, Washington would place an advertisement in the *Pennsylvania Packet* as well as other papers offering all or parcels of his lands "on three tenures: First, until Jany. 1795, and no longer; Second, until Jany. 1795, renewable every ten years forever; Third, for 999 years."

To other inquirers he offered to lease property closer to Mount Vernon, "for a good price and ready money," to encourage "a number of useful Husbandmen and Mechanicks to settle among us." At the same time, ironically, a ballad, "The Emigrant's Farewell," had appeared in England, observing that with the coming of peace, settlers impelled by economic need would reluctantly leave the mother country for such opportunities as Washington's fertile parcels promised. In the song's quatrains a prospective emigrant to "Columbia," an allegedly empty land where the "Fair Ohio floats upon her oozy bed," bids a doleful farewell to his "Dear native plains," consoled only by the likely benefits of productive life abroad and his newly won liberty. The General's vast properties, close to Mount Vernon and weeks of travel away, would keep him busy on his return home.

December 12–15, 1783

8

ARTS AND ENTERTAINMENTS

Tributes kept coming, threatening to overwhelm Washington's two remaining aides. On December 12, Washington received a commendation from the officers of the City and Liberties militia of Philadelphia. Inland from the Delaware but not absorbed by the city to its south, the Northern Liberties had been laid out by William Penn and was in the city street network. (Morris's mansion and farm were within the northwest border of the Liberties.) The area would be annexed only in 1854. Also, according to the Philadelphia *Independent Gazeteer*, the Philadelphia merchants' association "had an elegant entertainment prepared for General Washington at the City Tavern, as a fresh proof of their respect. . . . On this truly festive and happy occasion, toasts and sentiments were given. . . . The evening was closed with a ball, at which were present a very numerous and brilliant company of ladies and gentlemen."

Washington might have wondered how many of the ladies had danced—and perhaps more—at balls with British officers during their occupation of Philadelphia and how many of the merchants who chose to remain in the city had fattened their prospering accounts from the King's purse. From September 26, 1777, to June 18, 1778, more than two hundred shops were closed as their patriot proprietors fled and the Congress relocated westward to the town of York. Nevertheless, the city thrived.

The British had lived well indeed. With little inclination to do battle against the Continentals in the countryside, they staged plays and organized balls. Fashionable ladies flaunted their charms before Howe's aide, the handsome Major John André, who was angling to become Sir William's adjutant general. Among André's achievements had been a "Mischianza," a gigantic twelve-hour-long farewell extravaganza for General Howe on May 18, 1778, at the lavish Wharton mansion on Fifth Street in suburban Southwark, below Cedar (later South) Street, which boasted a tree-lined park sloping down to the Delaware. The revels had included a party served by twenty-four black slaves in oriental dress, with silver collars and bracelets; a regatta from Market Street wharf, where a band played, a midnight banquet for 430 guests, and a ball.

At the toasts, heralded by redcoated trumpeters, the already-sodden company arose to sing "God Save the King." At eleven, deep in the festivities, a pyrotechnical display occurred that the British had not planned. Slipping in from Valley Forge, Captain Allen McLane and his scouts crept through the lines and set fire to a length of felled-tree barricades. Answering guns boomed, and the silken-clad ladies cringed. Howe's officers assured guests that it was part of the entertainment. The dancing resumed. The feast continued. But thirty days later, Howe having relinquished command to Lieutenant General Sir Henry Clinton, the British abandoned Philadelphia, which was militarily useless anyway, to return to New York City.

Six years had passed. At the elaborate parting entertainment for Washington, the General, elegant afoot, danced minuets and reels with Philadelphia gentlewomen and asked no embarrassing questions about how they occupied themselves during Howe's memorable year. (Washington had learned to dance at fifteen, paying three shillings ninepence to attend a dancing school, and ever after enjoyed showing off his ballroom graces. Philadelphia's social elite, despite the city's Quaker ambience, were members of the exclusive Dancing Assembly, founded in 1748.) The first dolls imported from England since the war had already arrived, expensively attired in the latest London styles, and dressmakers were copying the costumes for chic belles in rich brocades and taffetas, with hoops standing out on both sides but flattened front and back. Local milliners were devising soigné "Gainsborough" hats topped by tall feathers.

Except for Washington's party, few men were in military dress. Modish males now wore narrow capes, long in the back, over short coats, with striped stockings and pointed shoes below their breeches. Large fortunes had been made during the war, both legitimately and less so, up and down the thirteen colonies. With the perspective of a bachelor neither pursuing ladies nor outfitting them, a Boston physician, Dr. Arthur Lee, complained to a friend that newly affluent Americans were "employ[ing] their wealth in a manner not very consistent with that unostentatious virtue which ought to animate our infant republic."

At the dinner before the ball, still insulated from changing vogues by his buff and blue uniform, Washington had been lauded for his "illustrious example of a citizen, called by a free people to the exercise of supreme command, and, after having so eminently contributed to effect a mighty revolution, which has raised his country to empire, returning with dignity to a private station, with the universal esteem and applause of his fellow citizens." His withdrawal from high position seemed even more extraordinary than his captaincy.

Diplomatically fudging the facts, Washington thanked the "Merchants of Philadelphia" in "the last time I shall have the honor of seeing you in my official character," for their "punctuality . . . in raising their proportion of Taxes for support of the War, and their chearfulness in affording every other assistance in their power," which were (if true) "marks of Patriotism which deserve the warmest acknowledgments." He had not felt that way when many were dragging their feet or supplying the occupiers. Some wealthy Quaker merchants had been unwilling, on pacifist principles, to lend money to support the war. Still, a few would close their eyes and proffer the money to Robert Morris personally. Late in 1776, for example, he had needed funds for Washington's intelligence service, and the Continental Congress could not even be asked to appropriate funds to pay spies. Approaching a well-to-do Philadelphia Quaker, Morris made known his need for five hundred golden guineas. "How can I, friend Robert, who am a man of peace," asked the worthy in a broad-brimmed black hat, "lend thee money for the purposes of war? Friend George is, I believe, a good man and fighting in a good cause; but I am opposed to fighting of any sort." Morris softened the old man's scruples about a personal loan, and he went out to his garden and spaded up a sack of gold coins, which found its way to the commander in chief.

On another occasion Morris approached a prosperous

Philadelphia Quaker with slightly fewer scruples. "Robert," the merchant asked cautiously, "what security canst thou give?"

"My note and my honor," said Morris. "Thou shalt have it," said the Quaker to Morris's surprise, and a few hours later, when Morris had the funds in hand, he wrote to Washington in a rare exuberant mood, "I was up early this morning to despatch a supply of fifty thousand dollars to your Excellency. It gives me pleasure that you have engaged the troops to continue; and if further occasional supplies of money are necessary, you may depend on my exertions, either in a public or private capacity."

It was seldom that easy. In October 1777, a committee of influential Friends had met with Washington himself to express Quaker condemnation of warfare, not excepting the American struggle for independence. Now, with peace, the fragile new nation again needed the help of the moneyed of every persuasion, and Washington promoted—in their interest, he implied—"a wise and just system of policy" to be adopted by all the states, for only then "will national faith be inviolably preserved, public credit durably established, the blessings of Commerce extensively diffused, and the reputation of our new-formed Empire supported. . . ."

His last business day in Philadelphia, his busiest, was Saturday, December 13. Washington received and responded to effusive addresses from the organization of city and county magistrates, the already venerable American Philosophical Society, "the Clergy, Gentlemen of the Law, and the Physicians of the City of Philadelphia" (representing the learned professions), and the trustees and faculty of the College of Philadelphia, to be chartered as the University of Pennsylvania in 1791. The university, founded by Benjamin Franklin and then at

Ninth and Market streets, had awarded him, in absentia, the honorary degree of Doctor of Laws.

Now, in person, Washington could thank the college for the academic honor. He also used the occasion to offer a sweeping new—perhaps Humphreyesque—restructuring of his closing peroration in keeping with his doctorate. "May the Revolution," he declaimed in a mouthful of verbiage to which his malfunctioning false teeth were almost certainly unequal, "prove extensively propitious to the cause of Literature; may the tender plants of Science which are cultivated by your assiduous care under the fostering influence of Heaven, soon arrive at an uncommon point of maturity and perfection, and may this University long continue to diffuse throughout an enlightened Empire, all the blessings of virtue, learning and urbanity."

That he—or Humphreys—continued to refer to "Empire" (as others often did) may seem puzzling. Did Americans still consider the new nation to be related in some way to the British Empire from which they had separated themselves, or did it merely suggest a nation of impressive scope? In Philadelphia, the newly erected, plain-style Free Quakers Meeting House at Fifth and Arch streets had just set into its north gable a stone tablet that proclaimed, puzzlingly,

> Erected in the YEAR
> of OUR LORD 1783
> of the EMPIRE 8

To Washington and others it seemed a figure of speech suggesting the sprawling continuity of the former colonies, which Americans expected confidently would expand at least to midcontinent—to the distant Mississippi, an area conceded by Britain in the treaty of peace in lieu of empty American claims to any part of Canada. The term would remain in the reservoir of his correspondence and his speechmaking. Washington would use it again the same day in his response to the learned professions, referring to their role "in the preservation of the Liberties, as well as the augmentation of the happiness and glory of this extensive Empire." Three years later he would prophesy, "However unimportant America may be considered at present, . . . there will assuredly come a day, when this country will have some weight in the scale of Empires."

Still determined to be home by Christmas, he acknowledged his honorary membership in the American Philosophical Society—another Franklin initiative, founded in 1743—by referring to Mount Vernon as "the philosophic retreat to which I am retiring." To Lafayette he would describe his hopes of becoming "a private citizen on the banks of the Potomac, and under the shadow of my own Vine and my own Fig-tree, free from the bustle of a camp and the busy scenes of public life." There he expected to be, soon, "solacing myself with those tranquil enjoyments, of which the Soldier who is ever in pursuit of fame, the Statesman whose watchful days and sleepless nights are spent in devising schemes to promote the welfare of his own, perhaps the ruin of other countries, as if this globe was insufficient for us all, and the Courtier who is always watching the countenance of his Prince, in hopes of catching a gracious smile, can have very little conception." He was, so he anticipated, "retiring within myself; and [I] shall be able to view the solitary walk, and tread the paths of private life with heartfelt satisfaction. . . . I will move gently down the stream of life, until I sleep with my Fathers."

Death was a part of everyday life in his time, and such fancies were unsurprising and without gloom. A local poet, beginning his verses about every freeman's bosom beating with joy on news of peace, had closed with the now-maudlin

> *Great WASHINGTON! supporter of our Cause!*
> *With affluence blest, and calm domestic joys:*
> *When time devouring levels him with dust,*
> *Th' immortal part may shine among the just.*

More and more, Washington discovered, he longed for his domestic sanctuary. He would repeat his impossible dream in many letters before and after Christmas, for in Philadelphia, as before in New York, he was beset by entreaties as well as burdened with encomiums. Both represented the inevitable. He was bombarded with applications from former colleagues and associates, both civilian and military, for his good offices in obtaining postwar employment. The "peace establishment" had been downsized to almost nothing, and gentlemanly occupation in government was hard to find. In most cases he was reluctant to intervene, but he offered most men who solicited his services his signed recommendation to be employed by them as they could. The importuning would continue when he returned home. Further appeals already awaited him at Mount Vernon.

No American name meant more than his, not even that of the venerable Dr. Franklin, who was a godlike figure in France. Washington would even receive a transatlantic request for his portrait from Friedrich-Christoph, Graf zu Solms und Tecklenberg, who characterized himself as an old soldier who had served the rulers of Saxony and Poland. Solms had fought under the likes of Frederick the Great, he explained. In his castle at Königstein, Solms hung the portraits of great soldiers, and was *"le plus sincere Admirateur de l'Illustre Wasington."* The General understood almost no French, and less German, but succumbing to Solms's flattery, he would arrange for his portrait by English-born Philadelphia artist Joseph Wright to be copied and sent to Saxony through the good offices of Robert Morris. Wright, Washington confided to Solms, was thought "to have taken a better likeness of me, than any other painter has done. His forté seems to be in giving the distinguishing characteristics with more boldness than delicacy. . . ."

Joseph Wright was the son of Philadelphia Quaker sculptor and waxworks artist Patience Lovell Wright, who from London had secreted messages intended for Franklin in Paris and for revolutionary leaders in America in the hollows of her wax heads. The deception foiled British naval searches. Young Wright had left London late in 1782. After study at the Royal Academy and early portrait commissions from American sympathizers in Paris and London, at twenty-six he returned on the ill-fated *Argo*. When it ran aground approaching Boston, Wright lost to the Atlantic his portrait of Franklin and another of his mother that were to display his skill, but he persuaded Washington to pose for a head-and-shoulders portrait and a life mask in plaster of Paris to be used to fashion a bust.

Claiming reluctance to endure a face mask, Washington told the visiting Elkanah Watson (a courier to Franklin) that the artist "oiled my features over; and placing me flat upon my back upon a cot, proceeded to daub my face with the plaster. Whilst [I was] in this ludicrous attitude, Mrs. Washington[, then visiting at Rocky Hill,] entered the room; and seeing my face thus overspread with the plaster, involuntarily exclaimed [in alarm]. Her cry excited in me a disposition to smile, which gave my mouth a slight twist . . . that is now observable in the busts which Wright afterward made." Amid Washington's muffled laughter the plaster was hurriedly removed—the only hurried action the very deliberate Joseph Wright was known to have taken.

Washington would have to prod Wright further through Morris about copying the portrait, suggesting, "As he is said to be a little lazy, you would oblige me by stimulating him to the completion. By promise, it was to be done in five or six weeks from the time I left Philadelphia." Solms would receive his half-length portrait of a stern, Roman figure in uniform jacket and scarf, that July. Washington paid all the costs.

Later the General, then a civilian, had mixed feelings about posing in classical garb, which he would not do for Wright. Writing to Jefferson about plans for yet another statue in his honor, he wondered whether the marble Washington would wear a toga, as was "the taste of connoisseurs." He proposed "some little deviation in favor of the modern costume, . . . which has been introduced in painting by Mr. West." The General understood that Benjamin West's realism "is received with applause, and prevails extensively." But in Jean-Antoine Houdon's celebrated bust, for which the sculptor crossed the Atlantic in 1785 to do his sittings, Washington is traditionally Romanized.

By December 8, although far away in London, where she was apparently living in St. James's Square with her daughter Phoebe and son-in-law John Hoppner, a rising portrait painter, Patience Wright had learned of Joseph's success, and thanked Washington. Although she was so acclaimed in England despite her Yankee sympathies that she was politically untouchable— Patience Wright was a greater artist although not the entrepreneur that was her successor Madame Tussaud—she saw her son's Washington portrait as likely to be her family's greatest commercial success. "Honoured Sir," she wrote in her self-taught spelling, and with a strong hint of approaching Christmas,

> I most heartly thank my god for sparing my life to see this hapy day—I joyne with all my friends in the pleasing prospect that Posterity will see, and behold the Statue of the man who was apointed by his Contry, and the Voice of the Enlightened Part of mankind to be the great general to save the Liberties of the Christian Religion and Stop the Pride of old England.—and by his truly great and noble Example in all human Vertues he has Restord *Peace* on Earth, *good will* toward mankind. . . .

She added her appreciation for Washington's encouraging her son's "genii" and hoped that she would receive a copy of Joseph's bust, for fashioning her hero in waxwork. "It has been for some time the wish and desire of my heart to moddel a likeness of generel Washington. Then I shall think my self arivd at the End of all my Earthly honours and Return in Peace to Enjoy my Native Contry."

Her letter did not arrive until December 12, 1784, a year later. Washington responded that he hoped the bust would reach her and give employment to her "rare and uncommon gifts." It would be "an honour done me." He invited Mrs. Wright to Mount Vernon, as "I should be proud to see a person so universally celebrated." But on returning from a visit to John Adams, the first American minister to England, apparently to arrange a voyage home, she fell and was seriously injured. On February 25, 1786, she died in London.

Despite a week in Philadelphia, Washington had not seen everyone to whom he wanted to say his farewells. Former general Anthony Wayne, the hero of Brandywine, had remained on duty in the South even after Yorktown, reoccupying Charleston after the British weighed anchor for home. Just retired in November, he was home in Chester County, ill, and unable to visit Washington, who could only write a parting note. Benjamin Franklin, feeble now in his late seventies, had not yet come home. He had been one of the three American commissioners—and the key figure—in Paris for the peace negotiations. Although promised by Congress that he would be able to return once the agreement was signed, as indeed it had been earlier in September, he was still awaiting his recall. Communications across Atlantic distances were slow, and uncertain, and on the day after Christmas, Franklin would write impatiently to remind Congress of his anxiety to be back in Philadelphia. Still, he would not receive authority to return until May 1785. A hitch might develop in activating the treaty.

Since Sunday was kept free from official duties, Washington could prepare to leave. He also managed to write further business letters, one to the gallant Marquis Charles Armand-Tuffin, who had been second in command to Lafayette in the final campaign against Cornwallis. The marquis, a wealthy aristocrat now thirty-three, had come to America after being forced to resign his royal commission when he wounded a cousin of Louis XVI in a duel. Armand had asked Congress to give to his legion some "lands on the other side of Ohio, in the proportion which has been promised to the army in general" and offered to buy land there "on a proportion of his half pay." When Congress had not been forthcoming and his troops were being disbanded, he wrote in his fractured English that he regretted "to not fight [further] for a cause more personal to his Excellency, general washington—happi indeed would I be at this instant where sheding all my blood, my soul leaving this world would glorify with the honor of having served my heroe." Since he was "not so fortunate, & already to[o] far in my career to change my profession," he sought Washington's help to be reinstated in the French army. He also wanted, "when your Excellency come to philadelphia, . . . certificats for some of the officers of the legion who have served with credit and may draw with advantage [in France] from their good conduct when attested by your Excellency."

Washington responded warmly that "Among the last acts of my public life, none afford me more pleasure than to acknowledge the assistance I have received from those worthy men whom I have had the honor to command, and whose exertions have so much contributed to the safety and liberty of my Country." Armand-Tuffin's zeal and bravery, as described in graphic detail by Washington in a letter of recommendation, was a litany of personal courage from Valley Forge to Yorktown. On returning to France from Philadelphia, Armand-Tuffin rejoined the king's *cavalerie* and rose to colonel, fighting with the royalists after the revolution in 1789 and recognized by the pet monkey perched on the croup of his horse.

"We are much employed here," Robert Morris wrote to Elias Boudinot, "in shewing the most affectionate marks of our strong attachment to the Commander in Chief." As that week was ending, Washington dismissed the small party of provost guards that had accompanied him since West Point, paying them "two or three months [salary]" which he would later try to extract from Morris and his hard-pressed Comptroller of the Treasury. Only the states themselves, in control of their own money, appeared always to have enough for their own purposes.

On December 2 the Pennsylvania legislature had even appropriated six hundred pounds, a very substantial sum, for an "extremely noble" triumphal wood and canvas Roman-style arch, with two side arches for pedestrians, from which "a constant succession of fine fireworks"—seven hundred rockets—were to be launched as "public demonstrations of joy" when the peace treaty was formally ratified by Congress. Forty feet high and fifty feet wide, it was to be erected over the rather open western end of Market Street, between Sixth and Seventh streets, "in order that the Citizens may have an Opportunity of viewing and examining the Exhibition with the greatest Convenience and Satisfaction to themselves."

Wryly, Gouverneur Morris would write to Alexander Hamilton that the arch was the idea of strict Philadelphia Quakers who would not bring art into their own homes, yet "wished to serve both their Class and their Principles." It was to be decorated by paintings and Latin inscriptions in the "antient" manner under the supervision of "the ingenious" Captain Charles Willson Peale. (He had served with the City Militia in the Christmas crossing to Trenton, at Valley Forge, and at Germantown.) According to the *Pennsylvania Gazette,* "Those figures that are finished have afforded the highest satisfaction to all who have seen them. Among them is a striking likeness of our justly beloved Commander in Chief."

While in Philadelphia, Washington had traveled to Peale's long, narrow studio and gallery at Third and Lombard streets, near the southern border of the city, to pose under the painter's skylight, the first in America, on Wednesday, December 10, for the grand victory arch. Peale depicted the General, in a transparency to be backlit, as the twelfth of a symbolic thirteen images. Acquainted with the Assembly's specifications, the

General understood very well how he was to be portrayed, and for the occasion had no objections to being romanized as Cincinnatus, whose precedent he was paralleling. To Francis Hopkinson, Washington would concede his vanity-gratifying weakness for portrait sitting, writing whimsically yet frankly, "Now, no dray moves more readily to the Thill,* than I do to the Painters Chair."

Peale's instructions, approved by the Assembly on December 2, after a committee including Clement Biddle and Gunning Bedford, Jr., had reported its advice in detail, were precise:

XII
On the Dye of the Pedestal, upon the right Hand in passing through the Centre Arch, *Cincinnatus,* crowned with Laurel, returning to his Plough—The Plough adorned with a wreath of the same—The Countenance of *Cincinnatus* is [to be] a striking Resemblance of General Washington,
VICTRIX VIRTUS
Victorious Virtue

Twelve hundred candles were to glow behind the portraits, and as the signal shot for the fireworks sounded, an enormous figure of Peace was to be released atop the arch. To ensure that it would be viewed without interference by rowdies, the Assembly also resolved that "Any Boys, or others, who disturb the Citizens by throwing Squibs or Crackers, or otherwise, will be immediately apprehended and sent to the Work-house." The night scheduled for the celebration was set as January 22, 1784,

---

*The shafts of a wagon between which a dray horse was harnessed.

to follow ratification of the definitive Treaty of Peace. (It would be approved on January 14, 1784, and proclaimed in Philadelphia at the Court House by the City Sheriff on the twenty-second.)*

Washington would not see his new portrait. On Monday morning December 15, the General left Philadelphia with a much reduced escort. There seemed still sufficient days remaining to arrive home by Christmas, although that depended upon completing his business with Congress. For a short distance south, through the port of Chester, close to the Delaware state border, his dwindling party was accompanied by the City Troop of Horse, with French ambassador de La Luzerne mounted on his right and John Dickinson riding on his left. Bumping ahead of them were Robert Morris and his wife, Molly, in a carriage. (Curiously, Morris's diary fails to mention anything but financial transactions that date.)

Observing the departure was Street Commissioner Jacob Hiltzheimer, a former City Militiaman, who wrote in his journal of "the illustrious" Washington, "Now I think it is not likely that I shall have the honor of seeing that great and good man again, and therefore, do sincerely congratulate him on the no-

---

*As darkness fell on the 22nd and street lamps were being lit to begin the ceremony, the first rocket to ignite set fire to the paintings, and the remaining fireworks atop blew up. "In 10 minutes," Peale wrote to a friend in London after three weeks' confinement in bed, "the work of much pains & study was consumed to ashes." In the confusion of horses, carriages and people, many spectators were injured and an exploding rocket stick killed the sergeant in charge of the fireworks. Peale fell, breaking a rib. His clothes were afire and he rolled in the fresh snow to douse them. The celebration of peace turned into a night of consternation and sorrow. But triumphal arches would appear again in America. Another disposable one was erected in New York, at Madison Square, to honor Admiral George Dewey when he returned from Manila after the war with Spain in 1898, and a vast parade of soldiers, sailors and bands passed beneath it.

ble resolution he has made, not to accept public office hereafter, but to pass the remainder of his days in private [life]. This is undoubtedly the surest way to preserve the honors he so justly acquired during the late war."

George Washington's Homecoming
Map 3 - Elkton to Mount Vernon

PENNSYLVANIA

MARYLAND

VIRGINIA

Susquehanna River

Head of Elk
(Elkton)

Lower
Susquehanna
Ferry

Joppa

Baltimore

Chester Town

Potomac River

George Town

Bladensburgh

Annapolis

Severn River

South River

Queens' Town

Alexandria

Mount Vernon

Pohick

Patuxent River

Chesapeake Bay

Choptank River

0   5   10   20   Miles

N
W   E
S

Douglas Greenfield

9

TOWARD ANNAPOLIS

Once the Philadelphia contingent had turned back, only Humphreys and Walker accompanied Washington, with the servants handling the General's carriages, each drawn by two horses. The once formidable honor guard had shrunk so visibly that as the commander in chief crossed into Delaware he was effectively if not officially already a civilian. By a recent act of Congress the former colony was no longer formally the "3 Lower Counties on Delaware" and had become "Delaware State." The population out to greet him also thinned as the party cantered southward, but that was only because of far fewer residents in the tiny state, rather than receding adulation, or rugged weather.

Leadership required more than a bit of luck. Not since Tappan, in mid-November, had Washington encountered snow and ice. His escort had also encountered no breakdowns of wagons, horses gone lame, or untoward incidents along the way. The godlike aura about him seemed to be holding.

Riding hard, the party reached the outskirts of Wilmington

by darkness, which now came early. Waiting for them with lanterns on the high road overlooking the river, now broadening toward Delaware Bay, were the governor and his council, the attorney general, local officials, and a group of Washington's former officers. "Express" riders kept people at his next destinations apprised of his whereabouts (Washington tipped the horsemen); and on reaching the small port and market town, the only inhabited place larger than a village in the tiny state, the cavalcade was greeted by a thirteen-gun salute—"discharges of cannon"—and an elegant supper laid on in a tavern. Outside the inn, according to the weekly *Pennsylvania Packet*, the local citizenry "demonstrated their joy by making large bonfires."

The next day, December 16, Washington was greeted by local officials "accompanied by a number of respectable inhabitants" and patiently listened to an address read in the name of the burgesses and Common Council of Wilmington. The town clerk, Joseph Shallcross, declared that the General's "magnanimity" had been their "invincible shield on the most gloomy occasions" when they "sometimes shuddered at the prospect [of defeat]." He hoped that "even in the serene enjoyment" of Washington's retirement, "which will astonish mankind little less than the splendor and greatness of your services," his "parental consideration"—he was already widely acclaimed "the Father of his Country"—would be available to advise "our infant governments." In return, the General declared "that the genuine approbation of my fellow-citizens is far more satisfactory, than the most lavish encomiums could be." Although he was returning "to a long meditated retirement," he assured them, "tho' I shall no more appear on the great Theatre of Action, the Wellfare of our infant States can never be indifferent to me."

He would not have been indifferent to the tenor of an anxious letter written that day from Annapolis by Thomas Jefferson to fellow Virginia congressman (and lawyer) Edmund Pendleton, "We have no certain prospect of nine states in Congress and cannot ratify the treaty with fewer, yet the ratifications have to be exchanged by the 3rd of March." Although Washington's formal resignation required a quorum of states only for decorum, it was essential for the peace treaty, which stipulated, allowing for travel time across the Atlantic, that both parties had to sign it within six months of its date—September 3, 1783. Congress had scheduled its Annapolis session to begin on December 13, but the number of states with delegations assembled for the nation's business had started with six and diminished to five. To James Madison, Jefferson complained, "We have never yet had more than 7 states and very seldom that, as Maryland is scarcely ever present, and we are now without a hope . . . till February; consequently having six states only, we do nothing." Something, however, could be done. To change the rules for a quorum required a quorum. Congressmen appealed to colleagues to return in January, if only briefly, to make ratification legal. A few would return sooner, for the Washington ceremony, then quickly go home again for Christmas.

Washington's course through Philadelphia and the outpouring of esteem for him had given John Dickinson, whose relations with the General had once been strained, a delicate question to broach to the Pennsylvania delegation. However much Washington wanted to sequester himself as a Virginia planter, his fame among his countrymen realistically precluded that. Whatever he intended, he was likely to remain the overwhelming personality in American life, and the new nation needed him. Although he had asked for no pension or expense account in retirement, his public out-of-pocket expenses were likely to be considerable. While Washington was passing through Wilmington on December 16, Dickinson as Pennsylvania's chief executive raised the issue with the state's representatives in Congress:

> Gentlemen,
>
> Tho' his Excellency General Washington proposes in a short time to retire, yet his illustrious actions & Virtues render his Character, so splendid and venerable that it is highly probable, [that] the admiration & Esteem of the world may make his Life in a very considerable Degree public, as numbers will be desirous of seeing the great & good Man who has so eminently contributed to the Happiness of a Nation. His very services to his Country may therefore subject him to improper Expences, unless he permits her Gratitude to interpose.
>
> We are perfectly acquainted with the Disinterestedness & Generosity of his soul. He thinks himself amply *rewarded* for all his Labors & Cares by the Love and prosperity of his Fellow Citizens; it is true, no Rewards that they can bestow can be equal to his merits. But they ought not to suffer those Merits to be burthensome to Him. We are convinced, the People of Pennsylvania would regret such a consequence.
>
> We are aware of the Delicacy with which this subject must be treated; But relying upon the Good sense of Congress, We wish it may engage their early attention.

The proposal would arrive at Annapolis before Washington. Aware that he was due before Congress shortly, the Pennsylvania delegates met to discuss a response to Dickinson. Although they could not see how Washington could escape, utterly, into private life, they predicted that the retired hero would accept no pension, nor even a grant of "an annual sum to indemnify him for expenses, which may arise from the particular situation he must be in." Replying from Philadelphia, Dickinson would urge nevertheless that "the proposition in some general Form" be brought to the consideration of Congress. "The Mode must be left to their politeness, & the substance to their generosity to determine. There appears to us no Impropriety, in the general's table being kept up during his Life, as Commander in Chief." Perhaps evading a Washingtonian refusal, Congress did nothing.

Leaving Wilmington on the morning of the seventeenth, the General was again in the saddle, en route on the post road to Baltimore via Hollingsworth's Tavern at Elk Head, Elk Ridge Ferry, and the Lower Susquehanna Ferry. There the horses and wagons turned southwest, skirting the muddy inlets from the Chesapeake Bay, misty in approaching twilight. In winter many of the tidal rivers froze over, and horse-drawn vehicles could cross on the ice, but it was too early in the season for that. Another traveler from Philadelphia to Baltimore on the way to Congress, William Ellery of Rhode Island, wrote from Annapolis on December 19 of "the badness of the roads," that "some of our horses were in frequent danger of being overset."

Lieutenant Colonel Walker recorded Washington's stops, avoiding inns that were mere grog shops and seeking ferriage where necessary. For the only time in the journey, at Baltimore Town no welcoming party met them. In the darkness, exhausted, the riders put up for the night at Grant's Tavern, where they were expected. On rising the next morning they accepted the usual congratulatory addresses from local citizens, who claimed "a universal joy in your Excellency's arrival" and acknowledged Washington's "eminent services and superior abilities." He had managed "the glorious and happy conclusion of an unequal, precarious and bloody war, through which you have . . . established the liberties and independence of your native country, and gained to yourself the unrivalled appellation of its most illustrious citizen." As always he was wished "domestic tranquillity" and, piously anticipating the hereafter, that Heaven then "grant the only adequate reward of your exalted merit." In reply, Washington praised their "flourishing town" (then smaller than Charleston, South Carolina) and wished the Marylanders "encrease" and "universal prosperity."

That Thursday evening he was entertained at a dinner at the Fountain Inn, on Light Street, where the Baltimore Dancing Assembly met in the shadow of the adjacent Methodist church. A ball at the Inn, where he was guest of honor, would go on until two in the morning of the nineteenth. Delighting his primped and powdered hostesses, the indefatigable Washington danced in turn with all of them. Guests tried to edge closer to him, literally—however gloved—to touch him, to acquire some emanation of his godlike gravitas. While he could clasp hands with a bewigged gentleman in velvet breeches, and even embrace longtime comrades in arms, for women the only equivalent, as social custom dictated, was to partner the General at a discreet distance while the band paced them about.

As no one was eager to leave, Washington had to explain when the clock struck two (the scheduled close) that he had to hurry on later that morning, for he had promised to have Christmas dinner with Mrs. Washington. The music stopped, and the company made its reluctant exits.

All that Washington could be certain about at his Mount Vernon Christmas to come—if he could arrive in time—was that some holiday music played at convivial Virginia Christmases past was certain to greet him no longer. Sung at plantation festive boards had been a loyal anthem, to the tune of "God Save the King," which hailed,

Fame let thy Trumpet sound.
Tell all the World Around.
Great George is King.

Once that fell from favor during the war, a small hired band— on occasion the exotic combination of a French horn and two violins—would accompany guests in "Liberty Songs," followed by minuets and country dances. Christmas carols did not yet exist in America, or in Britain, and there were no Christmas trees, as the custom was still largely Alsatian, having originated in Strassburg, from which it would spread into Saxony and Prussia during the Napoleonic wars.

American Dutch lore in New Amsterdam, the future New York City, recalled merrily a generous if mythical and elfish fourth century Sante Klaas (St. Nicholas, Bishop of Myra, in present-day Turkey), whose gift-giving day for children was De- cember 6. The custom sometimes merged with Christmas. The ship in which the first Hollanders arrived to settle the island of Manhattan even had St. Nicholas for its figurehead. *Rivington's Gazeteer* (as it was then titled) had noted on December 23, 1773, the recent anniversary of the beneficent saint, "otherwise called St. a Claus," a rare early reference to his veneration by "descendants of the ancient Dutch families."

December 6 was a feast day, as was Christmas, but in the New England colonies dour Puritan officials had long tried to suppress even that, as "frolicking" was condemned. In Cromwellian years, Christmas itself had been solemnly stricken from the calendar of holy days. On December 24, 1652, Parliament had legislated that "No observance shall be had of the five and twentieth day of December, commonly called Christmas Day; nor any solemnity used or exercised in churches." Across the Atlantic in Boston, Puritans believed that fallen and sinful people—as all were—would be wicked to celebrate such an anniversary. In 1659 a law was passed in the Massachusetts Bay Colony that "Whosoever shall be found observing any such day as Christmas . . . either by forbearing of labour, feasting, or any other way, . . . shall be subject to a fine of five shillings."

In the Quaker ambience of Philadelphia, the socially prominent Elizabeth Drinker classified citizens as those who "make no more account of [Christmas] than another day," those who were conventionally religious, and the many others, who "spend it in riot and dissipation." In liberated New York City the holiday began to be celebrated so rowdily that in 1785 the state legislature reinstated the colonial statute, extending its coverage to forbid the firing of guns, rockets, squibs, and other fireworks on Christmas Eve and New Year's Eve.

As an anonymous versifier in *The Virginia Almanack* explained, Christmas for its clientele was a time for food and fellowship, when Southern gentry, as opposed to their gloomy northern brethren, would

> *drink good wine and eat good cheer*
> *And keep their Christmases all the Year.*

How much and what kind of good cheer depended upon the openness of the squire of the manor. To Colonel William Fitzhugh of Stafford County, to the southwest of Mount Vernon, it had meant "three fiddlers, a jester, a tight-rope dancer, and an acrobat who tumbled around." Field hands and even one's slaves—Washington himself had about two hundred when he left for the war—were also permitted to dance and sing on Christmas, but only in their own quarters. *The Virginia Almanack* for 1775, the first year in many Christmases that Washington was away from home, prophesied, "We may expect to hear of a great Mortality among the Hogs, Sheep, Geese, Capons, Turkies, &c. . . ." Children would haunt the kitchens, hoping to acquire a pig's bladder to use as a balloon.

Also according to the *Almanack*, "Much good liquor"—from lemon punch and "cyder" to toddy, spiced ale, porter, and wine—"will likewise be consumed this month, [and] a Deal of Coals and Wood." That the practice emanated from the highest quarters in the home country was clear from the abrupt shutting off of debate on the American crisis in the House of Commons toward the close of the year before the rebellion began. Objecting, Edmund Burke criticized Lord North, the prime minister, for adjourning Parliament just "to eat mince pies, and drink Christmas ale."

In Virginia as well as in England, a formidable "Christmas Log" was the primary holiday symbol. Little had changed since the Anglican divine Robert Herrick, his piety in low key, had written in his "Ceremonies for Christmasse" (1648),

> *Come bring, with a noise,*
> *My merrie, merrie boys,*
> *The Christmas log to the firing;*
> *While my good dame she*
> *Bids ye all be free,*
> *And drink to your heart's desiring. . . .*

As tradition had it that no work was to be performed until the log burned completely down, servants and even slaves would boldly sprinkle it with water to retard its extinction.

Among the squirearchy in Virginia, Christmas Day often began not only with "Guns fired all around the House," as a guest at one plantation noted just before the revolution, but with early morning eggnog preparatory to an alcohol-fortified fox hunt that attracted both rich and poor revelers from around the county, and their dogs, in an orgy of "yelping, howling, shouting, singing and laughing." Exhausted, they returned to their midafternoon Christmas dinners. On his first postwar Christmas at home, Washington, who loved the hunt, almost certainly settled only for dinner.

Although not a profoundly religious man, Washington had married Martha on "Twelfth Night or Old Christmas Eve" twenty-four years earlier, very likely as the conclusion to the festive season. His Christmases were also more hearty than solemn. While church attendance was required of Anglicans by Virginia colonial statute, it was unenforceable. As a leading citizen in the area, Washington had become a vestryman at Pohick Anglican Church near Mount Vernon in 1765 and contributed annually to its upkeep but apparently never took communion (although Martha did), and he would retire from that office when he withdrew from other public positions. He employed rhetorical devices like "Almighty Being" and "Providence" in his addresses and eschewed theological specifics while recognizing impalpable powers beyond his grasp and the popular desire for prayer.

Even in the South, Christmas was not a legal holiday, as it would become in some states by the 1830s. Official revelry was slower to come in the north of the nation, inhibited by joyless Puritans and Quakers. Yet it was in the north—in New York—that the *Troy Sentinel* published, on December 23, 1823, at first anonymously, Clement Clarke Moore's high-spirited ballad "'Twas the Night Before Christmas or [An] Ac-

count of a Visit from St. Nicholas."* It quickly became insep-
arable from the holiday season, which it almost reinvented.
The sentimental Victorian Christmas, abetted also by Charles
Dickens and Washington Irving, was still remote, and other
than the flaming log in the principal fireplace the advent of
the colonial festival was marked by "Christmas Guns." In a
plantation custom already a century old, Christmas morning
was celebrated by the firing at dawn of a small field piece by
local slaves, accompanied by much happy shouting—it announced several days of freedom from work. Not permitted
powder or firearms, it was their rare opportunity to make an
acceptable loud noise. It had little to do with Christmas.
Slaves had inherited tribal traditions that some kind of very
loud banging drove off evil spirits.

If lacking a small ceremonial cannon, their masters sometimes would fire hunting rifles in the air as a holiday greeting
that would carry across the long distances to neighboring es-
tates. Then it became time for servants to venture, one by one,
into the private family quarters with the excuse to do something special, but presenter and recipient both understood that
it was to receive a "Christmas box"—actually some small coins,
often a "bit," or sixpence. A few servants were special and received more than small change. After Washington's return he
discharged Philip Bater, a likeable and efficient gardener, for
drunkenness, but when Bater timidly reapplied for the job,
Washington had second thoughts. He drew up a probationary

---

*Not entirely original, Moore's more jaunty poem was probably inspired by verses in
the obscure, illustrated *The Children's Friend* (New York, 1821), in which on Christmas
Eve a bearded bishop called "Old Santeclaus" travels on a sleigh drawn by a single reindeer to distribute presents, usually toys, some placed in stockings left to fill, to all
good children while leaving "a long, black, birchen rod" for parents to employ on
naughty ones.

contract in which the gardener was not at any time to "suffer himself to be disguised with liquor, except on the times here-after mentioned. . . . [as follows:] four Dollars at Christmas, with which he may be drunk 4 days and 4 nights; two Dollars at Easter to effect the same purpose; two Dollars also at Whitsun-tide, to be drunk two days; a Dram in the Morning and a drink of Grog at Dinner or at Noon." There was no mention of Boxing Day, which in Britain was the day after Christmas. Servants were expected to work through the festive day before enjoying their belated holiday.

Early on Friday, December 19, Washington's Christmas progress toward Mount Vernon continued, still skirting the inlets from the Chesapeake and crossing the Severn River be-fore it widened. A few miles from the Maryland capital of An-napolis he was met by a welcoming party including, unexpectedly, General William Smallwood of the Maryland Line and General Horatio Gates, the victor at Saratoga but dis-credited after his blundering defeat, and retreat, at Camden, South Carolina in 1780. Gates had spent the next two years pressing for vindication at a court martial, and succeeding at it, although he had lost a third of his army, but his career after Camden had been only nominal. Smallwood was an equally unanticipated well-wisher. He, too, had been a failure at Cam-den, threatened to resign when placed under von Steuben, and remained in service afterward only in minor posts, raising troops and supplies in Maryland, where he had retired the month before. Washington would continue to encounter for-mer colleagues who were less than fervent admirers. Leader-ship meant making hard choices, and he had often disposed of rivals and failures by placing them where they could do as lit-tle harm as possible.

For the early arriving delegates, Annapolis proved, by comparison with Princeton (little more than a village) a far more hospitable place. David Howell of Rhode Island wrote to his friend William Greene, "The City stands on rising ground & looks into the Bay by a most beautiful prospect. The Severn runs by it on the North West & [Robert Creek and Carrol's Creek,] another river or creek on the other side—so that we appear to be almost surrounded by water. . . . There are no morasses, saltmeadows—or stagnant waters. . . . The State House & the House assigned for the President are spacious & eligantly finished." The five hundred homes included those of "wealthy land owners" for whom it was their "winter quarters," a place for their "diversions." Howell was told that "here is a play house, a ball-room & many good taverns, but there is no place of public worship."

While the Annapolis reception committee escorted Washington's party to George Mann's Hotel at the corner of Main and Conduit streets, thirteen further rounds of cannon fire confirmed the General's arrival. More formally, he would announce his own presence, writing early on December 20 (in Benjamin Walker's hand) to Thomas Mifflin, the new president of the Congress, "Sir: I take the earliest opportunity to inform Congress of my arrival in this City, with the intention of asking leave to resign the Commission I have the honor of holding in their Service. It is most essential to me to know their pleasure, and in what manner it will be most proper to offer my resignation, whether in writing or at an Audience; I shall therefore request to be honored with the necessary information, that being apprized of the sentiments of Congress I may regulate my Conduct accordingly."

Although Washington seemed to be offering alternatives to his appearance, he fully expected a public audience, and wanted one, to dramatize his yielding of military authority to the civil sector. As early as his farewell address to officers mustered out at Newburgh, on March 15, he had urged the men on their "sacred honor" to resist any attempts at Caesarism in "our common Country" and "to express your utmost horror and detestation of the Man who wishes, under any specious pretences, to overturn the liberties of our Country, and who wickedly attempts to open the flood Gates of Civil Discord. . . ." He would not be that man.

10

FINAL FAREWELL

Washington knew much about discord, and wanted none of it
to mar his leave-taking. Another old acquaintance, Thomas
Mifflin of Philadelphia, now presiding officer of Congress, had
been involved in the misnamed Conway Cabal late in 1777,
when Washington was mired in difficulties, his army barely intact. Horatio Gates, on the other hand, was then being toasted
as the hero of Saratoga, the general who had bested Sir John
Burgoyne. A shadowy conspiracy identified with the impetuous
Irish soldier of fortune Thomas Conway, the ambitious and
most junior of the twenty-four brigadier generals among the
Continentals, had intrigued to undermine the luckless Washington. To Congress, Conway claimed that although the General was an estimable Virginia gentleman, "his talents for
command of an Army . . . were miserable indeed." Plotting to
replace Washington with Gates, Conway's backers were Samuel
Adams, Richard Henry Lee, Dr. Benjamin Rush—and Mifflin.
They had circulated an anonymous manifesto accusing gullible
patriots of being "guilty of idolatry in making a man their God."

Although Conway was promoted to major general with the open sponsorship of his accomplices among the delegates, and Mifflin remained influential in the weak Congress, Washington had easily brushed aside the challenge. When Conway, the next year, was wounded in a duel and thought he might die, he wrote a melodramatic apology to Washington, confessing, "You are in my eyes the great and good man. May you long enjoy the love, veneration and esteem of these States, whose liberties you have asserted by your virtues." Then Conway, married to a French countess, returned to France, and a career in its army. Washington duly became the deity to Americans that the others had warned of, esteemed as de facto head of state.

Recognizing that he owed an address to the Maryland legislature in their capital city, the General renewed his calls for a stronger national government that could face up to its likely challenges. Downplaying any sense of urgency, the General Assembly (on December 22) would thank him for showing how "to value, preserve, and improve that Liberty" which his services had ensured and added, vaguely, "If the powers given to Congress by the Confederation should be found incompetent to the purposes of the Union, our constituents will readily consent to enlarge them." It was again clear to Washington that the plaudits he was receiving would not in themselves unify a confederation of self-interested states that assumed smugly that their challenges were now behind them.

Whatever Mifflin's long coolness toward his old adversary, he recognized overwhelming public opinion and made the appropriate gestures. On Saturday December 20, he dined amiably with Washington, inviting to the spacious house furnished to the president of Congress other delegates and officials of the state of Maryland. Impressed, one of the delegates at Mifflin's dinner, Elbridge Gerry of Massachusetts, wrote to his colleague Samuel Holten, who had returned home, that Washington "would retire to private Life a finished Character, for it may justly be said of him, he is a great, & a good Man."

The General learned that his letter to Mifflin had been read in Congress, and that body had resolved to give him a public entertainment on Monday December 22 and an audience the next day at noon to receive his resignation. Should a quorum of nine states not be seated, Congress had determined (evidently without a quorum yet on a roll call vote) that seven—all that had representatives on hand—would be "competent" to act on his retirement.

Ratifying the formal treaty of peace with Britain was a more serious technicality. When the Treaty of Paris was belatedly and finally signed, early in 1784, Congress sent Lieutenant Colonel David Solebury Franks, once Benedict Arnold's aide-de-camp, and Lieutenant Colonel Josiah Harmar, Anthony Wayne's deputy at Yorktown and now Mifflin's private secretary, separately, as insurance against the severity of winter weather across the North Atlantic, to exchange ratified treaties. The British were happy to receive the document, whatever the expired deadline.

Georgia, always the most dilatory state, had already notified the Congress that it would send no delegates during the winter months. Several others were wary of any attendance that might create an obligation to be taxed—"so careless," Thomas Jefferson complained, "are either the states or their delegates to their particular interests as well as the general good which would require that they be all constantly and fully represented in Congress." Although he was equating particular interest and

general good, some states viewed the two concepts very differ-
ently.

A committee of three—Thomas Jefferson, Elbridge Gerry,
and James McHenry—was named to stage every detail of Washington's audience. It was to be a piece of consummate theater:

1. President [of Congress] and members are to be seated
   and covered,* and the secretary to be standing by the
   side of the President.
2. The arrival of the General is to be announced by the
   messenger to the secretary, who is thereupon to in-
   troduce the General attended by his aid[e]s to the
   Hall of Congress.
3. The General being conducted to a chair by the secretary is to be seated with an aid[e] on either side,
   standing, and the secretary is to resume his place.
4. After a proper time for the arrangement of spectators,
   silence is to be ordered by the secretary, if necessary,
   and the President is to address the General in the
   following words: "Sir, The United States in Congress
   assembled are prepared to receive your communications."

   Where upon the General is to arise and address
   Congress, after which he is to deliver his Commission
   and a copy of his address to the President.
5. The General having resumed his place, the President
   is to deliver the answer of Congress, which the General is to receive standing.

---

*In English parliamentary tradition, members wore hats, and strict rules indicated
when they were to remove them. A Member's hat was worn to enter the chamber, and
donned when taking a seat. One wore a hat to vote, and bared the head only when
speaking. A hatless member could not be recognized by the Chair. One could also not
rise to a point of order without wearing a hat.

6. The President having finished, the secretary is to deliver [to] the General a copy of the answer, and the
   General is then to take his leave.

   When the General rises to make his address, and also
   when he retires, he is to bow to Congress, which they are
   to return by [rising and] uncovering without bowing.

On the morning of December 21, Washington received visits from further dignitaries at his hotel, very likely grateful that
the tedium of formal greetings, however flattering, was at an
end. To the mayor, council, and aldermen of Annapolis, he
replied, perhaps because it was a Sunday, in particularly pious
rhetoric. "I owe it," he declared, "to that Supreme being who
guides the hearts of all; who has so signally interposed his aid
in every Stage of the Contest and who has graciously been
pleased to bestow on me the greatest of Earthly rewards: *the approbation and affections of a free people.*" And he closed with the
hope, "May the Almighty dispose the heart of every Citizen of
the United States to improve the great prospect of happiness
before us. . . ."

Afterward he wrote a lengthy letter to Mifflin, for the Congress, appealing that many officers "obliged to retire" and high
in his esteem sought appointments "on any Peace establishment that may take place." Washington had not wanted to remain in Annapolis as long as Congress had planned, but
Mifflin hoped for a reduced quorum on Tuesday. Recognizing
the importance of each word in his written resignation, he left
such subsidiary work for Humphreys and Walker as replies to
addresses and final letters for his signature as commander in
chief and began drafting himself the text he would deliver. Almost certainly he had a copy ready for Jefferson's committee to
use in preparing a formal response by the time he arrived in

Annapolis. Reviewing the statement, he went over his phrases "an affectionate and final farewell" (to the Congress) and his taking "ultimate leave" of public service and chose to expunge some of the finality. He was going home, but although he was nearly fifty-two and yearned for Mount Vernon, was he really to bar the door to all further calls upon him? The sustained adulation, amounting to near worship, and his recognition of the unstable state of the infant republic, were shifting his obduracy by a degree or two. He struck out *and final* and *ultimate*. The long farewell had made a difference to his, and the new nation's, future.

Far, now, to the northeast, the *Boston Gazette and Country Journal* published on the twenty-second the now familiar "The Heroes Come!" anthem to "mighty Washington" on the reoccupation of New York. Much as he had attempted to leave public life, he had no rival in reputation. No one else in any former colony so symbolized the new nation. On another page the *Gazette* published a satirical column of "Intelligence Extraordinary" from London which included a "LOST" column. What appeared lost was

A large tract of land called AMERICA: whoever shall bring it back again to Mrs. Britannia, shall receive thirteen stripes reward.

Charles Thomson considered Annapolis a town "where Pleasure holds her Court," where there was an abundance of "turkies, fine fish and oysters." In his Rhode Island rigidity, David Howell deplored "the amusements of this place such as plays, Balls, Concerts, routs, hops, Fandangoes & fox hunting," and the tone of Annapolis that Howell considered profligate was borne out that Monday when an "elegant and profuse" din-

ner and ball were sponsored by the newly reelected governor,
William Paca (a signer of the Declaration of Independence), and
arranged by hotelier George Mann. In a Christmas Day letter to
Gunning Bedford, Jr., soon to be Delaware attorney general,
James Tilton of Delaware described the proceedings as "the
most extraordinary I have ever attended." The squat State
House, adorned by an oversized cupola visible from the bay,
was made festive, and "Between 2 and 3 hundred Gentn: dined
together in the ball-room."

Among the guests were Mynheer Pieter van Berckel, the en-
voy of Holland,* the Chevalier de La Luzerne, the French minister, and—more surprisingly—Sir Robert Eden and Henry
Harford, who in republican affability forgot, in James
McHenry's description, their "opposite principles and manners." Eden, the last royal governor of Maryland, and Harford,
the young heir to the former provincial proprietor, the 6th Earl
of Baltimore, had returned from England to air property claims,
but dined and danced with the others, and, James Tilton wrote
to Gunning Bedford, Jr., "Master Harford was so gay as to say
that he would show away** if the *State* would give him any
thing to do it with. . . . The number of cheerful voices, with the
clangor of knives and forks made a din of an extraordinary nature and most delightful influence. Every man seemed to be in
heaven or so absorbed in the pleasures of imagination, as to

---

*Transatlantic travel was so chancy and unpredictable, especially east to west against
contrary winds, that it took the Dutch minister 16 weeks to sail from Holland to
Philadelphia. He was miffed when he wasn't formally greeted. From Princeton, late in
October, Elias Boudinot, then President of Congress, wrote regretfully, "We feel ourselves greatly mortified that our present circumstances in a small Country village prevent us giving you a reception more agreeable to our wishes. But I hope these
unavoidable deficiencies will be compensated by the sincerity of our Joy on this occasion."

**In the nautical use of the verb it meant spreading one's sails to the wind.

neglect the more sordid appetites, for not a soul got drunk, though there was wine in plenty and the usual number of 13 toasts. . . ."

A grand dinner with thirteen toasts was expected wherever Washington was feted, and Mann's catering bill bears out the conviviality. He invoiced Congress $664.75 for the food and drink, the beverages itemized as ninety-eight bottles of wine, two and a half gallons of "spirits," and nine pounds of loaf sugar and twenty-five limes to enhance the liquor. Other charges were for musicians, waiters, "attendance in the Barr" before dinner, twelve packs of cards for postprandial play while others danced, eight pounds of candles, and one pound two shillings and sixpence for "cleaning the Rooms" afterward. It was a heroic occasion.

No one would have confused "His Most Christian Majesty" in the third toast with George III, and the curious reference to Louis XVI of the French may have been intended as an indirect swipe at the former ruler of the American colonies. American gratitude to France remained so strong that it was usually guaranteed two toasts in the symbolic enumeration of the thirteen:

1. The United States
2. The Army
3. His Most Christian Majesty
4. The United [Provinces of the] Netherlands
5. The King of Sweden
6. Our Commissioners abroad
7. The Minister of France
8. The Minister of the Netherlands
9. Harmony, and a flourishing Commerce, throughout the Union
10. May Virtue and Wisdom influence the Councils of

the United States; and may their Conduct merit the
Blessings of Peace and Independence.
11. The virtuous Daughters of America
12. The Governor & State of Maryland
13. Long Health and Happiness to our illustrious General
eral

Tilton also reported to Bedford that there was an additional
toast "given afterwards by the General [in response] which you
should be acquainted with." It was "Competent Powers to Congress for general Purposes." (To unify the nation, Washington
persisted at every opportunity to promote more authority for
Congress.) After each toast, a signal was given for approving
cannon fire outside (symbolically, as always, there were thirteen cannon) to punctuate the cheers and applause, and the
State House shook. So much pandemonium persisted inside
and out that the drinking of toasts hardly raised the emotional
level.

Following the dinner Governor William Paca and the General Assembly hosted the inevitable ball for Washington. Excluded from the alcoholic preliminaries, women elegantly
attired (in a contemporary description) in "stiff stays, [and]
hoops from six inches to two feet on each side" arrived at the
hall (now being cleared) in black high-heeled shoes for the
dancing. They entered, Tilton wrote, "like a crab, pointing their
obtruding flanks end foremost." Really fashionable women arrived for the ball with their hair in the *Dress à l'Independence*,
which prescribed thirteen curls at the neck.

A band played reels, then slowed the pace occasionally to
minuets. According to Tilton, "To light the rooms every window was illuminated. . . . The company was equally numerous, and more brilliant, consisting of Ladies and Gentm: Such

was my villainous awkwardness, that I could not venture to dance on this occasion." He felt like "such a mortified whelp."

Washington opened the ball with gusto, whirling round Martha Rolle Maccubbin, twenty-two, considered one of the most beautiful women in Maryland, and certainly one of the most wealthy.* From the sidelines, Tilton observed, the General "danced every set, that all the ladies might have the pleasure of dancing with him, or as it has since been handsomely expressed, *get a touch of him.*" Yet a touch by custom was always indirect. Not only was a stately minuet or even a rapid, partner-exchanging reel danced at a hoop-skirted distance—as always, all dancers discreetly wore gloves.

Early on the morning of December 23—Washington was getting little sleep but did not seem to be the worse for it—the General looked over a draft response to an address offered in the names of the Governor and Council of Maryland. It had been prepared by Benjamin Walker for delivery in writing. (His aides were also getting little sleep.) The General had already declared to the General Assembly, in a David Humphreys draft, that it was "only by wise and equitable Measures, that I can derive any personal satisfaction, or the public any permanent advantage from the successful issue of the late Contest." Now he added his wish that "the same spirit of Justice and Patriotism" which actuated them during the war would lead to "the future prosperity of the State."

Impulsively, it seems, he wrote still another letter, in his own

---

*Her husband, James Maccubbin, wealthy in his own right, had just inherited half the estate of his uncle, Charles Carroll of Duddington, considered one of the richest men in Maryland. Maccubbin would become Judge of the Orphans' Court of Anne Arundel County.

hand, to Baron von Steuben, from whom he had parted hurriedly in Philadelphia. The Baron had meant too much to him to have only been involved in the flurry of farewells there. Now, just before Washington returned at noon to the State House, where Congress would receive him with all their elaborate trappings, he wrote, in the idiosyncratic spellings of the time,

> My dear Baron:
> Altho' I have taken frequent opportunities, both in public and in private, of acknowledging your great zeal, attention, and abilities in performing the duties of your Office; yet I wish to make use of this last moment of my public life, to signifie in the strongest terms my entire approbation of your conduct, and to express my sense of the obligations the public is under to you, for your faithful and meritorious Services. . . .
> This is the last Letter I shall ever write while I continue in the service of my Country; the hour of my resignation is fixed at twelve this day; after which I shall become a private Citizen on the Banks of the Potomack, where I shall be glad to embrace you, and to testify [to] the great esteem and consideration which I am yours. . . .

Von Steuben, the "first teacher" of the American army, had become a citizen of Pennsylvania in March 1783 and would be made a citizen of New York in July 1786. Careless about his expenditures while anticipating about sixty thousand dollars he claimed optimistically from Congress for his military services, he would run into financial distress. Finally in 1790 he received a $2,500 annual pension instead of the lump sum he claimed, and only a mortgage on acreage given to him in New York kept him going in style until his death in 1794.

As Washington left for the State House, servants at Mann's Hotel packed his bags and trunks and groomed his horse and those of his aides, posting them outside the door for efficient departure. With the draft of the arrangements and his retirement address and his original commission from Congress (engrossed on parchment) in a coat pocket, the General appeared just before noon. Delegates were present from Masachusetts, Rhode Island, Pennsylvania, Delaware, Maryland, Virginia, North Carolina, New Hampshire, and South Carolina, only twenty members in all, seated and with hats perched on their heads.

An attendant greeted Washington's party and then returned with Charles Thomson, the Secretary of Congress. Escorted by Thomson, Washington, in his buff and blue military uniform, passed through and was directed to a seat near Thomas Mifflin. Walker and Humphreys, also in uniform, stood on either side of the General. Attendants then reopened the doors to the chamber and eminent guests—Abiel Foster of New Hampshire described them as "the Governor & Council, the Senate & House of Assembly . . . and the principal Gentlemen & Ladies of the City"—entered. The men, Tilton wrote, clustered along the walls—"filled all the avenues" and "crouded below stairs." Then the doors to the small gallery above were opened, and invited ladies took seats "as full as it would hold."

When, in 1824, John Trumbull painted, for the Capitol Rotunda, his huge and ambitious *The Resignation of General Washington, 23 December 1783,* he sent out letters asking for assistance in tracing portraits, busts, and drawings of the participants. He had not even been in the country at the time of the ceremony, embarking from Portsmouth, New Hampshire to paint in London earlier that December. Jonathan Trumbull, his father, a patriot former governor of Connecticut, had asked his son, then twenty-seven and a wartime officer like Jonathan, Jr., to remain home, but John Trumbull had argued, "You appear to forget, sir, that *Connecticut is not Athens.*" He had learned about the event while working with Benjamin West and on returning home began to plan the canvas. Later he would write to James Madison, who had not been present, that he had taken the liberty of introducing him into the occasion to represent (a painter's license, he explained) all four presidents from Virginia. From a balcony looking down on the scene, although they were not there either, are Martha Washington and three of her grandchildren.

Art has often redrawn history, as with the iconic canvas of Washington crossing the Delaware by Emanuel Leutze (1851), executed in Dusseldorf and showing the General riskily standing up in his small boat and a flag aboard not yet publicly displayed. Trumbull's Yorktown painting shows Cornwallis surrendering his sword to Washington although the ceremony had been delegated to General Charles O'Hara. In Benjamin West's *Death of Nelson,* the admiral expires on deck off Cape Trafalgar amid a crowd of officers and crew, although he died far less dramatically in a tiny cabin below; and the grungy sailor boy in New York who unfurls Washington's flag at Fort George, in the centennial illustration of the event in the once popular *Frank Leslie's Illustrated Newspaper,* is well-groomed and mature beyond boyhood.

When the audience crowded into the State House had hushed, Mifflin turned to Washington with "Sir, the United States in Congress assembled are prepared to receive your communications." As the General arose and bowed, members removed their three-square cocked hats in lieu of a return bow, then replaced them. James McHenry recalled that Washington's hand shook as he read from his text, and that at times "his voice faultered and sunk, and the whole house felt his agitations." When he "recover[ed] himself, he proceeded . . . in the most penetrating manner."

Mr. President,

The great events on which my resignation depended having at length taken place; I have now the honor of offering my sincere Congratulations to Congress and of presenting myself before them to surrender into their hands the trust committed to me, and to claim the indulgence of retiring from the Service of my Country.

Happy in the confirmation of our Independence and Sovereignty, and pleased with the opportunity afforded the United States of becoming a respectable Nation, I resign with satisfaction the Appointment I accepted with diffidence. A diffidence in my abilities to accomplish so arduous a task, which however was superseded by a confidence in the rectitude of our Cause, the support of the Supreme Power of the Union, and the patronage of Heaven.

The Successful termination of the War has verified the most sanguine expectations, and my gratitude for the interposition of Providence, and the assistance I have received from my Countrymen, encreases with every review of the momentous Contest.

While I repeat my obligations to the Army in general, I should do injustice to my own feelings not to acknowledge in this place the peculiar Service and distinguished merits of the Gentlemen who have been attached to my person during the War.

Washington had controlled his emotions to that point, but according to McHenry he then had to grip the paper with both shaking hands to steady it enough to proceed.

"It was impossible," he continued, alluding to the aides at his side as well as others now relieved from active duty,

> [that] the choice of confidential Officers to compose my family should have been more fortunate. Permit me, Sir, to recommend in particular those, who have continued in Service to the present moment, as worthy of the favorable notice and patronage of Congress.
>
> I consider it an indispensable duty to close this last solemn act of my Official life, by commending the Interests of our dearest Country to the protection of Almighty God, and those who have the superintendence of them, to his holy keeping. Having now finished the work assigned me, I retire from the great theatre of Action; and bidding an Affectionate farewell to this August body under whose orders I have so long acted, I here offer my Commission, and take my leave of all the employments of public life.

From his coat pocket, Washington withdrew the parchment that was his appointment from Congress as commander in chief, dated June 15, 1775, and returned it ceremoniously to Thomas Mifflin. For his audience it was a moment of consummate drama. For its implications it was also, however early it occurred in American history, the most significant address ever delivered to a civil society.

Although Tilton deprecated Mifflin's reply as "a set speech," it was a moving farewell, largely written by Thomas Jefferson. The arrangements committee had a copy of Washington's address in advance, in order to prepare a response, and Jefferson had told Gerry and McHenry to examine his draft and "Be so good as to handle it roughly and freely and make it what it should be." It might be "too warm," he apologized, blaming "an exalted esteem." In the end the draft was probably shortened by Jefferson himself. "I have been obliged to obliterate and blot," he confessed, after excising specific wartime episodes like Washington's "revival of our hopes by recrossing the Delaware" and "finally the capture of Cornwallis." The draft appears to have been discussed in advance by the Congress also, as some alterations in the hand of its secretary, Charles Thomson, seem to represent amendments inhouse before working copies were made for Mifflin and Washington.

At the podium in the State House, Mifflin replied to the hushed crowd in Jefferson's draft acknowledgment of Washington's address, reading from the fair copy prepared by McHenry. Congress, he declared, receives "with emotions too affectionate for utterance, the solemn resignation of the authorities under which you have led their troops with success through a perilous and doubtful war." The General, so Mifflin conceded, had "conducted the great military conflict with wisdom and fortitude, invariably regarding the rights of the civil powers." He had been able to gain "the love and confidence of your fellow citizens" as he achieved their "freedom, safety and independence. . . . But the glory of your virtues will not terminate with your military command—it will continue to animate [the] remotest ages." For Washington had "defended the standard of liberty in this new world—having taught a lesson useful to those who inflict, and those who feel oppression."

Closing with a peroration that moved his audience as much as had Washington himself, he employed language that James Madison would describe as "the shining traces" of Jefferson's pen:

We join with you in commending the interests of our dearest country to the protection of Almighty God, beseeching Him to dispose the hearts and minds of its citizens to improve the opportunity afforded them of becoming a happy and respectable nation. And for *You,* we address to *Him* our warmest prayers, that a life so beloved, may be fostered with all His *care*—that your days may be happy as they have been *illustrious,* and that He will finally give you that reward which this world cannot give.

The General bowed again to Congress; members rose silently and removed their hats in respect, and Washington retired with his aides.

"The farewell of General Washington," David Howell wrote, "was a most solemn Scene. . . . And many testified their affectionate attachment to our illustrious Hero and their gratitude for his Services to his country by a most copious shedding of tears." Concurring, McHenry recalled, "The spectators all wept, and there was hardly a member of Congress who did not drop tears." Yet according to the exacting Marylander, despite the moving language written for Mifflin, he read his reply "without any show of feeling, though with much dignity." To Benjamin Harrison, the Virginia governor, Jefferson wrote (the next day) only that it was an "affecting scene" which Harrison would read about in the press, and that Washington's address "was worthy of him."

Very likely Jefferson wrote in much the same manner, but immediately after the event, to Francis Hopkinson. The evidence exists only in the "Summary Journal," where Jefferson recorded his letters, and in Hopkinson's reply. In the quiet aftermath of Washington's departure he wrote a long letter to his friend in Philadelphia, noting among its subjects "Buffon's theory—Rittenh's orrery for the k. of Fr." The two had only recently become close, sharing confidences, when the Hopkinsons began caring for the widowered Jefferson's daughter Patsy. France and things French seemed always to come to mind after Yorktown—a chord also struck during the last toasts for Washington.

The extraordinarily learned Jefferson also had his mind on the sky. As a token of thanks to Louis XVI, Jefferson had persuaded the American Philosophical Society to commission the polymath astronomer David Rittenhouse (who fabricated Washington's spectacles) to create an orrery for the king, a geared apparatus with balls attached to the ends of branches of different lengths that, in rotary motion, demonstrates the positions and movements of bodies in the solar system. (Unfortunately, the preoccupied Rittenhouse, also State Treasurer of Pennsylvania, would never complete the orrery.) Possibly in connection with the project, Jefferson had been reading about George Louis Leclerc de Buffon's system of astronomy in the two volumes of his *Histoire naturelle* and used the occasion for a jesting synopsis.

When thanking Jefferson extravagantly "for the Pains you have taken" to explain Buffon, Hopkinson enclosed, separately, a satiric "Christmas Gambol" and wrote playfully of England as a sun "in a fluid State," and France "in the Eccentricity of her political movements" as a comet that had collided with it and "struck off" a now-independent America, which had carried away with its dislodged mass some of the solar atmosphere—English culture, laws, and language—and, as "a new Planet in the System," was now moving into "an Orbit of its own." Still fixated on where the national capital would be placed, Hopkinson suggested that planets cool first at their north, which accounted for the migration of Congress southward. Jefferson's "Ingenuity," Hopkinson bantered, "will easily investigate the whole, and apply the most minute Parts of Monsr. Buffon's solar System to the American Revolution."

By the afternoon of the long letter to Hopkinson, Washington was migrating even further southward himself, seemingly out of politics.

From Richmond, the Virginia capital, a former army captain at Valley Forge and now an assemblyman and lawyer, John Marshall, would write to James Monroe in language far more effusive than he would ever employ as Chief Justice of the United States, "At length the military career of the greatest Man on earth is closed. May happiness attend him wherever he goes. May he long enjoy those blessings he has secured to his Country. When I speak or think of that superior Man my full heart overflows with gratitude. May he ever experience from his Countrymen those attentions which such sentiments of themselves produce." A generation later, his Virginia compatriot James Madison told John Trumbull, who painted him and the absent Martha Washington into his canvas anyway, that it was "a glorious action . . . as a contrast to the military usurpations so conspicuous in history."

Reporting the event, the *Boston Independent Chronicle and Universal Advertiser* published in an adjoining column, as it thought appropriate, "Verses occasioned by General Washington's arrival in this city, on his way to his Seat in Virginia," from the *Freeman's Journal* in Philadelphia, Philip Freneau's newspaper (and his unsigned poem). Seventeen stanzas celebrated upon "the great unequal conflict past," and Washington as "the Genius of these Lands" who "disdains all vulgar fame" and before whom "Despots trembled at your name." Again the Cincinnatus image was dominant, very likely as Washington would have wished as his legacy:

> *Now hurrying from the busy scene—*
> *Where thy Potomack's waters flow,*
> *May'st thou enjoy thy rural reign.*
> *And every earthly blessing know:*
> *Thus HE who Rome's proud legions sway'd*
> *Return'd and sought his sylvan shade.*

As the General stepped into an anteroom, preparing to depart, Mifflin dismissed all spectators before formally adjourning the assembly. To David Humphreys, Mifflin whispered warmly as Washington left the dais that "if any thing should occur to me in consequence of what had been suggested in favor of the Gentlemen of General Washington's [official] family who had continued with him to that moment," Humphreys should "communicate it to him in a Letter" and Mifflin "should take great pleasure in laying it immediately before Congress." (Mifflin would be of little help. When Washington became President, he would appoint Humphreys Minister to Portugal.)

Then the General, a private citizen after more than eight years, "step[p]ed into the room again, [and] bid every member farewell." He shook hands with each, and said goodbye. That done, he "rode off from the door, intent upon eating his Christmas dinner at home. Many of the spectators, particularly the fair ones[,] shed tears, on this solemn and affecting occasion."

Later that afternoon, Mifflin penned short messages to the governors of the thirteen states to confirm the proceedings. "I have the honor to inform you," his letter to Thomas Dickinson went, "that this day at twelve o'clock His Excellency General

Washington had a public audience of Congress, resigned his Commission and took his leave of all the employments of public life. . . ."

McHenry's description of the event filled most of an anguished love letter to the beautiful Margaret Caldwell of Philadelphia, written that evening. He began with reproaches that since the previous Friday he had "counted the minutes of each day" waiting for a letter from her that never came. He had been on such "a rack of suspense," McHenry confessed, that "I was to assist in writing our answer to General Washington's resignation—but I am unfit for this purpose." Still, he offered his "sketch of the scene," explaining, "were I to write you a long[er] letter I could not convey to you the whole. So many circumstances crowded into view and gave rise to so many conflicting emotions. The events of the revolution just accomplished—the new situation into which it had thrown the affairs of the world—the great man who had borne so conspicuous a figure in it, the act of relinquishing all public employments to return to private life—the past—the present—the future—the manner—the occasion—all conspired to render it a spectacle inexpressibly solemn and affecting." Then he closed with, "But I have written enough. Good night, my love. . . ." All would be well. He married Miss Caldwell little more than two weeks later, on January 8, 1784.

Governor Paca and his party accompanied Washington as far as the South River ferry, below Annapolis. Twilight came much too soon in late December, no matter how hard the horsemen would ride, for them to reach the Potomac before darkness. Up the Hudson, still the North River to Lieutenant Greenman's soldiers, discharge papers had finally reached their headquarters from Albany and they would be released on

Christmas Day. "Fixing to discharge our men," Greenman wrote, "and waiting for the Muster Master and Lieutenant [Joseph] Wheaton, who had gone to . . . procure Some Shoes and other Cloathing for our naked* men—but [he] returned with only a pair of Shoes for each man. . . ." For transport the usual practice was to give each man an expense outlay for getting home of a penny a mile.

Although a civilian now, Washington was also entitled to going-home expenses, and he continued to itemize them, even the gratuities to men at his final overnight stopping place for "assisting with my Bags," which included his camp chest and a hair trunk. It was only after arising the next morning that his party approached the ferry landing on the broadening "Potomack" below Alexandria. ("Ferriages" were noted down as $1.40.)

Visible, now, as they disembarked on the Virginia side and proceeded toward the slopes of Mount Vernon, were the vistas of his beloved country seat and the columned riverfront portico on which Martha, so Washington must have assumed, watched and waited. The road to the house, however, ran from Alexandria inland, rather than along the river. The woods were thick on both sides and his wagons had to scale two steep hills. Then came the plantation's fields, orchards, and meadows and a pair of wooden gates. The curving drive through the broad meadow beyond led to the main house. Still nearly a mile distant, Mount Vernon looked inviting nevertheless, with its three shuttered doors in the white west front and its many green-shuttered windows, now candlelit. It was Christmas Eve.

---

*In Colonial times, *naked* could mean being devoid of clothing proper to one's station, rather than nudity.

11

CHRISTMAS AND AFTER

Washington's family Christmas remained private and almost entirely unrecorded. In his own six-foot-six bed, in the early morning darkness of Christmas Day (Washington always arose at five), he realized, gratefully, "I was no longer a public man, or had anything to do with public transactions." The uniform he had hung in his wardrobe the night before—a coat of deep blue, with buff trim and brass buttons, and his buff waistcoat and breeches—remained there. In his cupboard, he had hung his battle sword in its black leather scabbard and its white leather belt, with silver plate engraved "1757," a relic of his service in the frontier wars against the French. He had completed a farewell journey that he described simply, in a letter to Jonathan Trumbull, Jr., one of his secretaries almost to the end, as a "Scene . . . of festivity, congratulation, Addresses, and resignation."

More emotionally, Washington would write to Henry Knox (and similarly to others) in words that suggest John Bunyan's *The Pilgrim's Progress,* a work he very likely could not have escaped as a youth, "I feel now . . . as I conceive a wearied Traveller must do, who, after treading many a painful step, with a heavy burden on his shoulders, is eased of the latter, having reached the Goal to which all the former were directed; and from his House top is looking back, and tracing with a grateful eye the Meanders by which he escaped the quicksands and Mires which lay in his way; and into which none but the All-powerful guide, and great disposer of human Events could have prevented his falling."

Martha Washington would write to Boston author Mercy Otis Warren six years later that she "little thought when the war was finished, that any circumstance could possibly happen to call the general into public life again"—that she "anticipated that from that moment [of his return] they should have grown old together, in solitude and tranquillity:—this, my dear madam, was the first and fondest wish of my heart."

What his convivial Christmases at home were like once he had settled in again can be pictured from a letter written to his former aide-de-camp David Humphreys a few holiday seasons later when he deplored being "deprived . . . of your aid in the Attack of Christmas Pyes. We had one yesterday on which all the company (and pretty numerous it was) were hardly able to make an impression."

He had returned, he realized, just in time—and not only because it had been Christmas Eve. As he wrote to Charles Thomson, on January 22, nearly a month later, "We have been so fast and locked in Snow and Ice since Christmas, that all kinds of intercourse have been suspended. . . ."* "We have had no account, from the Potowmack since your departure," Thomas

---

*In Philadelphia, the Delaware iced over on Christmas Eve and no vessels were able to sail upriver until March 13, 1784.

Mifflin wrote respectfully on December 28 from Annapolis, "and have been under great Apprehensions that the Journey was disagreeable and difficult, from the snow which fell on Wednesday night." Edward Hand of Pennsylvania would write to his friend Jasper Yeates in Lancaster two days later, as Congress still sat three states short of a quorum, of "a succession of deep snows." Washington had barely made it home before winter had seized the land.

Recalling his last day before the public, Washington queried Thomson, "If my Commission is not necessary for the files of Congress, I should be glad to have it deposited amongst my own Papers. It may serve *my Grand Children* some fifty or a hundred years hence for a theme to ruminate upon, *if they should be contemplatively disposed.*"

Thomson would respond hopefully, "With respect to your *commission* I have to inform you that previous to the rec[eip]t of your letter it had been [a matter] in agitation among the members [of Congress] to have an Order passed for returning it to you in a gold box. A motion has accordingly been made to that effect, w[i]ch was received with general approbation, and referred to a comm[itt]ee to be drawn up in proper terms. The comm[itt]ee have not yet reported. But I have not the least doubt of its being returned to you in a way that will be satisfactory and I heartily wish, that this sacred deposit may be preserved by your children and children's children to the latest posterity and may prove an incentive to them to emulate the virtues of their worthy and great progenitor."

As Washington settled gratefully into retirement, in *Bailey's Pocket Almanack for 1784* Philip Freneau wrote that

> *In Vernon's groves you shun the throne,*
> *Admir'd by kings, but seen by none.*

Stirred by the General's renunciation of command, John Trumbull wrote to his brother from London that it had earned "the astonishment and admiration of this part of the world. 'Tis a Conduct so novel, so inconceivable to People, who, far from giving up powers they possess, are willing to convulse the Empire to acquire more." Both dimensions of the General's implicit rejection of a crown would be recalled by ex-emperor Napoleon when in exile on remote St. Helena. "They wanted *me* to be another Washington," he explained, defending his own imperial ambitions, but circumstances ruled out his republican faith. When still only Consul of France, late in 1799, he had even ordered the army into mourning for ten days when Washington died, and made a speech eulogizing the man who had "put his country's freedom on a sure basis." But Napoleon became, Lord Byron would charge, "the Washington of worlds betray'd," while, in the poet's sardonic "Ode to Napoleon Buonaparte," the squire of Mount Vernon remained

> . . . *the first—the last—-the best—*
> *The Cincinnatus of the West,*
> *Whom Envy dared not hate.*
> *Bequeath the name of Washington,*
> *To make man blush there was but one.*

Despite the resolution moved in the Congress by Hugh Williamson that "his late Commission be returned to General Washington in a neat gold box," and its referral to a committee headed by Jefferson for appropriate language to accompany it, the commission was not returned in a gold box—indeed, not at all.

NOTES

Spellings in America would not be regularized until long after Noah Webster began publishing his "Spelling-Book," which became *A Grammatical Institute of the English Language*. Its first part appeared in 1783, the year of Washington's return to Mount Vernon. Webster's immensely influential *American Dictionary of the English Language* was published in 1828. Washington and his contemporaries would employ such now-curious spellings (as appear here) as *phinominy, charactor, oppertunity, chearful, encrease, perswade,* and *wellfare*. Later printings would often modernize Washington's spellings, creating new inconsistencies.

Dates recalled by participants are sometimes a matter of vagrant memory, often set down forty years later. It was a young and unlettered army—and citizenry. Lines from contemporary letters and journals were later freely altered in publication. Quotations, for example, from Jacob Hiltzheimer's complete diary as published are different in extracts than in the full diary.

Washington had carefully kept a diary earlier, but in the war years he abandoned that discipline, and the closest link we have to events are his letters and the letters and diaries of others, the expense accounts kept in his own hand and by his aides, and the less trustworthy press accounts. Martha Washington wrote few letters and burned most of her husband's letters to her.

Historians and biographers have also freely enhanced incidents, some from the suggestions of painters more interested in dramatic anecdote than fact. Mrs. Washington in some accounts is in New York for her husband's departure; children are raised up by their parents to see her, and she leaves on a barge with the General. Other accounts set her at a ball in Baltimore and at his resignation ceremony in Annapolis, although the firm evidence is that Washington had sent her home from Princeton in early October. Another imaginative account has Washington travel by sea directly home from New York. A modern biography even declares that Washington kept his retirement plans secret from Congress, to spring a surprise. The documentary evidence in every case proves otherwise.

SOURCES

The basic sources for Washington's letters and addresses, with identification of aides who drafted many of them for his signature, are *Writings of George Washington from the Original Manuscript Sources, 1745–1799*, ed. John C. Fitzpatrick, 39 vols. (Washington, DC, Government Printing Office, 1931–1944), *Papers of George Washington*, ed. W. W. Abbott, Dorothy Twohig, et al., Revolutionary War Series, vol. 8 and Confederation Series, vol 1. (Charlottesville, University Press of Virginia, 1992), and *Writings of George Washington*, ed. John Rhodehamel (New York, Library of America, 1997). William Spohn Baker's *The Itinerary of General Washington from June 15, 1775 to December 23, 1783* (Lambertville, NJ: Hunterdon House, 1970 [1892]) is a useful if spotty and incomplete reference largely taken from such contemporary newspapers as the *Pennsylvania Journal* and GW's writings. Unless otherwise identified later, Washington references and quotations are from these publications. Most letters by delegates to the Continental and Confederation Congresses are extracted from a magnificent edition by Paul H.

Smith et al., *Letters of Delegates to Congress 1784–1789*, vol. 21 (Washington, DC: Library of Congress, 1994). Specifically described here from their sources are exhibits from a major visual collection, *The Great Experiment: George Washington and the American Republic*, ed. John Rhodehamel (New Haven: Yale University Press and San Marino: Huntington Library, 1999). The myth and impact of Washington as a Cincinnatus figure are explored in Garry Wills's *Cincinnatus: George Washington and the Enlightenment* (New York: Doubleday, 1984). An essential reference work utilized here is Mark Mayo Boatner III's *Encyclopedia of the American Revolution* (Mechanicsburg, PA: Stackpole, rev. ed., 1994).

PREFACE

My wartime Christmases in Korea were in 1951 and 1952. See chapter 9 for the backgrounds of Clement Clarke Moore's "A Visit from St. Nicholas." For further detail on Cincinnatus, see the close of chapter 5.

1
BEGINNING THE END

On August 12, 1787 Washington wrote to John Augustine Washington, his nephew, that he expected imminent delivery of "the top for the Cupulo of the House, which has been left so long unfinished." Thus when he returned after the war, it was to a Mount Vernon without the now-familiar roof lines. Abigail Adams described GW to her husband in a letter, July 16, 1775, in L. H. Butterfield, *Adams Family Correspondence* (Cambridge: Harvard University Press, 1963). The Abbé Robin's admiring view of Washington, published as his *New Travels,* were extracted in the *Pennsylvania Gazette* in September 1783, furnished in translation by "I.H." It was reprinted in the *Salem Gazette* (Massachusetts) on October 2, 1783. John Adams's suspicion of power for generals is quoted by Catherine Drinker Bowen in *Miracle at Philadelphia* (Boston: Atlantic-Little, Brown, 1966). Talk about Washington as potential dictator appears in a letter from Ezekiel Cornell to Governor William Greene of Rhode Island, August 1, 1780, quoted by Merrill Jensen in *The New Nation: A History of the United States During the Confederation, 1781–1789* (New York: Knopf, 1962).

James Madison's unhappiness with dreary Princeton is described in a letter quoted in Edmond Cody Burnett's *The Continental Congress* (New York: Norton, 1964). That Martha Washington left the Princeton area for home on October 7, 1783 is confirmed in a letter from Congressman Samuel Holten to John Hancock, October 9, 1783, in *Letters of Delegates to Congress 1774–1789,* vol. 21 (see above). The Newburgh letter from Washington's generals to the Commander in Chief, November 15, 1783, was published in the *Pennsylvania Gazette,* November 26, 1783. The indifference of the states to both the Continental and the Confederation Congresses is detailed by Allan Nevins in *The American States During and After the Revolution, 1775–1789* (New York: Kelley [repr.], 1969 [1924]).

General Robertson's letter to Lord Amherst in London, June 12, 1781, on the seizure of the courier and his letters, is in Milton M. Klein and Ronald W. Howard, *The Twilight of British Rule in Revolutionary America: The New York Letter Book of General James Robertson, 1780–1783* (Cooperstown: New York State Historical Association, 1983). Statistics on Loyalists leaving New York were reported by Carleton in a letter to Lord North on November 29, 1783, reproduced in K. C. Davies, ed., *Documents of the*

American Revolution (Colonial Office Series) XXI, Transcripts 1782–1783 (Dublin: Irish University Press, 1981). The numbers are incomplete: more refugees boarded evacuation vessels after that date. Thousands more also went to Quebec, the West Indies, and England, and the Hessians returned to Germany. Again, Carleton's reports furnish reliable statistics.

Details on British maltreatment of prisoners of war are in Henry R. Stiles, *History of the City of Brooklyn* (Brooklyn: published by subscription, 1867). Biographical data on Carleton are largely from Paul David Nelson, *General Sir Guy Carleton, Lord Dorchester: Soldier-Statesman of Early British Canada* (Madison/Teaneck, NJ: Fairleigh Dickinson University Press, 2000). The proclamation of General Carleton and Admiral Digby outlawing outrages upon American ships appeared in most Eastern newspapers; the text here is from the *Boston Gazette.* Carleton's arrest of counterfeiters of Morris's banknotes is reported in the *New-Hampshire Gazette,* August 9, 1783.

The Reverend Odell's couplet, from his "The Congratulation," is reprinted in William Alfred Bryan's *George Washington in American Literature 1775–1865* (New York: Columbia University Press, 1952). The coffeehouse praise of Washington was reported in a dispatch from London dated November 20, 1784 in *The Providence Gazette and Country Journal,* March 6, 1784.

2
THE PRICE OF INDEPENDENCE

The *Memoir of Colonel Benjamin Tallmadge* was published posthumously in 1858 and reprinted in the series *Eyewitness Accounts of the American Revolution* (New York: New York Times, 1968). The royalist depredations of Ephraim Smith and William Cunningham were reported in New York papers and others as far away as the *Boston Gazette and Country Journal* (there on December 15, 1783). Washington's "Sett of Beggars" letter to Congressman Bland, April 4, 1783, is in the *Writings*, XXVI. Other documents are from editions described earlier.

3
TO NEW YORK CITY

Thomas Jones's curse on Washington is from his intemperate *History of New York During the Revolutionary War*, ed. Edward Floyd de Lancey (New York: New York Historical Society, 1879), printed for the first time with notes nearly a century after Jones had left it in manuscript. Both sides of Sir Guy Carleton's correspondence with Washington are in the *Papers of GW*. Many pages of GW's manuscript expense account book are reproduced in facsimile, with some satiric asides relating them to corporate accounting practices, in Marvin Kitman, *George Washington's Expense Account* (New York: Simon and Schuster, 1980). Costs so recorded are referred to throughout the text. The avoirdupois of Washington's staff, recorded by Colonel Cobb at West Point, is itemized in North Callahan, *Henry Knox: General Washington's General* (New York: Barnes, 1958). The complaint about the wintry weather in Nova Scotia appeared in *Gentleman's Magazine*, London, in the issue for August 1783. The *Journal of Lieutenant John Charles Philip von Krafft, of the Regiment von Bose, 1776–1784*, with an introduction by Thomas H. Edsall, was published in 1882 from the collections of and by the New York Historical Society. The contrast of GW with Grattan and Flood is quoted from a London dispatch in the *New-Hampshire Gazette*, December 5, 1783. What the DeWint mansion looked like inside and out, and Washington's stays with the Blauvelts, are described by Eliot Tozer in "Dutch Mansion Hosted Washington," *Early American Life,* August 2002. Judge Smith's diary entries, April through July 1783, are from L. S. F. Upton, *The Loyal Whig: William Smith of New York & Quebec* (Toronto: University of Toronto Press, 1969).

4

REOCCUPATION

Repeating more than overlapping each other are accounts of GW's week of reoccupation in the *New York Packet,* the *New York Gazette, Holt's Independent New York Gazette, Rivington's New York Gazette,* the *Pennsylvania Packet,* and the *Boston Gazette and Country Journal.* Largely extracted from them are scrappy accounts in Elizabeth Bryant Johnston, *George Washington Day by Day* (New York: Baker and Taylor, 1895). Useful summaries from which some details have been extracted here are in the *Report of the Joint Commission on the Centennial Celebration of the Evacuation of New York by the British* (New York: New York Historical Society, 1885) and Alvin F. Harlow's *Old Bowery Days: The Chronicles of a Famous Street* (New York: Appleton, 1931).

For Hercules Mulligan, see G. W. P. Custis's memoir annotated in chapter 5. Washington's letter to the Tory Andrew Elliot, December 1, 1783, is in Fitzpatrick, ed., *Writings of George Washington,* v. 27, 251–52.

Jeremiah Greenman's army journal is *Diary of a Common Soldier in the American Revolution, 1775–1783,* ed. Robert C. Bray and Paul E. Bushnell (DeKalb: Northern Illinois University Press, 1978). Sanitary conditions in the last days of occupied New York City are described in James H. Gallagher's *Yesterdays* in *Little Old New York* (New York: Dorland Press, 1929). The Roxburyite's colorful description of the column of civilian New Yorkers is from the *Norfolk County Journal* (Massachusetts), March 9, 1850. For the Abbé Robin, see chapter 1. John Trumbull's Fabian image of GW is in his extravagant post-Trenton "The Genius of America: an Ode" (1777–1778), in which the General is also "the godlike hero."

Reports of the flag-raising at Fort George, at least one at odds with apparent reality (see the text of the chapter itself), are from the Clinton Papers (New York Historical Society), the *Pennsylvania Gazette* and the eastern press in general, and *Frank Leslie's Illustrated Newspaper*, November 24, 1883. Trumbull's painting of the scene, in which he combines Fort George with the final embarking of the British, is described by him in his memoir, *The Autobiography of Colonel John Trumbull, Patriot-Artist 1756–1843*, ed. Theodore Sizer (New Haven: Yale University Press, 1953). The emphasis about Connecticut not being Athens is Trumbull's own. For General Alexander McDougall, see Roger J. Champagne, *Alexander McDougall and the American Revolution in New York* (Schenectady, NY: Union College Press, 1975).

William Smith's full diary is his "Historical Memoirs," in six volumes, in the New York Public Library. Volume 6 includes 1783 and takes him from New York to London. The Reverend Ewald Schaukirk's diary, ed. Joseph P. Tustin, is *Diary of the American War: A Hessian Journal* (New Haven: Yale University Press, 1979). The threatening "card" is quoted in Thomas Jones, *History of New York During the Revolutionary War*.

Robert Mills's design including GW atop the obelisk in a triumphal chariot is described by F. L. Harvey in the *History of the Washington Monument and the National Monument Society* (1903) cited by William Alfred Bryan in *George Washington in American*

Literature (New York: Columbia University Press, 1952). Francis Hopkinson's satirical works, including "A Summary of Some Late Proceedings in a Certain Great Assembly," are quoted in George E. Hastings, *The Life of Francis Hopkinson* (Chicago: University of Chicago Press, 1926). Franklin's enthusiasm about ballooning is from a letter in Albert Henry Smyth, ed., *The Writings of Benjamin Franklin*, vol. 9 (New York: Haskell House, 1968 [repr. 1907 ed.]). William Bingham's device for balloon traveling is quoted from his pamphlet by Robert C. Alberts in *The Golden Voyage: The Life and Times of William Bingham* (Boston: Houghton Mifflin, 1969). Jefferson's letter to Hopkinson, February 18, 1784, on ballooning is published in *The Papers of Thomas Jefferson*, vol. 6, ed. Julian P. Boyd et al. (Princeton: Princeton University Press, 1952). "The Flying Machine" postal service is referred to by Edmund Cody Burnett in *The Continental Congress* (cited earlier).

5
THE FIRST FAREWELL

The text of the Treaty of Paris as it arrived on the *Lord Hyde* is quoted from the *Pennsylvania Packet,* December 3, 1783. Biographical data about David Humphreys and extracts from his biography of Washington, here and in other chapters, are from Rosemarie Zagarri, ed. (with her introduction), *David Humphreys' Life of General Washington: With George Washington's "Remarks"* (Athens: University of Georgia Press, 1991). The correspondence between Washington and Lafayette on silverplate as well as other matters is found in Washington's *Papers* and, more conveniently, in Stanley J. Idzerda and Robert Rhodes Crout, eds., *Lafayette in the Age of the American Revolution* (Ithaca: Cornell University Press, 1983).

Descriptions of the earthquakes are from the local press and from Robert R. Livingston's letter to John Jay, November 29–30, 1783, in Richard B. Morris, ed., *John Jay. The Winning of the Peace. Unpublished Papers, 17801784, II* (New York: Harper & Row, 1980).

The quotation from the *Pennsylvania Journal* about the godlike Washington is from Richard Kenin and Justin Wintle, eds., *The Dictionary of Biographical Quotation* (New York: Knopf, 1978). The "just as we have images of God's saints" quotation is from *G. Washington: A Figure upon the* Stage (see chapter 5). The bust of St. George Washington in the Nicaraguan church at Itivas was reported in the *Portsmouth Journal of Literature and Politics,* New Hampshire, March 21, 1857. Lincoln's inaugural ring containing a fragment from Washington's coffin is in the National Museum of American History and also recorded in *G. Washington.* President McKinley's wearing of an inaugural ring containing a strand of Washington's hair is from Warren Zimmerman, *First Great Triumph* (New York: Farrar, Straus & Giroux, 2002).

Details about William Duke Moore's seal celebrating American independence are from the Washington *Papers,* which includes the Moore correspondence. Reports of the minor earthquakes impacting Philadelphia and New York are from the local press. The report of surprised British reaction to "quietude and safety" in the city is "An Evacuation Anecdote" published in the *Salem Gazette,* February 5, 1784. A list of the fireworks displays over New York harbor was reported in many eastern newspapers; the account here is from the *Boston Independent Chronicle and the Universal Advertiser,* December 12, 1783. The technology of contemporary fireworks is drawn from Ronald Lancaster et al., *Fireworks: Principles and Practice* (New York: Chemical Publishing, 1998), and George Plimpton, *Fireworks: A History and Celebration* (New York: Doubleday, 1984).

Rivington's reception of GW and apparent payoff from the General is described at length in George Washington Parke Custis's *Recollections and Private Memories of Washington* (New York: World, 1859). The titles of the books GW asked Colonel Smith to acquire for him in New York are listed in *New York City During the American Revolution: A Collection of Original Papers from the Manuscripts in the Possession of the Mercantile Library Association of New York City* (New York: privately printed for the Association, 1861). Catherine Snell Crary's "The Tory and the Spy: The Double Life of James Rivington," *William and Mary Quarterly,* January 1959, cites corroborating evidence in the New York Historical Society, in particular the manuscript journal of another Washington informant, Allan McLane. Freneau's verses on Rivington and later verses, mostly anonymous, extracted in further chapters, are reprinted from *The Newspaper Verse of Philip Freneau: An Edition and Bibliographical Survey,* ed. Judith R. Hiltner (Troy, NY: Whitson, 1986).

6
FRAUNCES TAVERN

Hamilton's request to retain a token commission and his initiating what would be a lucrative New York law practice, are in James Flexner, *The Young Hamilton* (Boston: Little, Brown, 1978) and Julius Goebel, Jr., ed., *The Law Practice of Alexander Hamilton,* vol. I (New York: Columbia University Press, 1964). Hamilton's full letters and Washington's disappointing response, November 6, 1783, are in the *Papers of Alexander Hamilton, 1782–1786,* vol. III, ed. Harold C. Syrett (New York: Columbia University Press, 1962). Willard Sterne Randall in *Alexander Hamilton: A Life* (New York: HarperCollins, 2003) claims "tradition in both families" (GW's and AH's) for Hamilton's being at Washington's side from the reentry into New York City to GW's farewell at Fraunces Tavern, but nothing in the documentary record or eyewitness recollection bears this out. Randall's own *George Washington* (New York: Holt, 1996) does not mention Hamilton as having any relations with Washington for much of the 1780s. Hamilton's closest associates on his return to New York City, Hercules Mulligan and Robert Troup, both wrote memoirs of him that are equally blank about this period except for his offer to defend Rivington when the printer was threatened with "taking the types away." See Nathan Schachner ed., "Alexander Hamilton as Viewed by His Friends," *William and Mary Quarterly*, April 1947.

Edmund Burke is quoted in Jerome R. Reich, *British Friends of the American Revolution* (London: Sharpe, 1998). Benjamin Franklin's will is dated June 23, 1789, just after Washington was inaugurated as president. Such toys as a "Tea Sett," now at Washington and Lee University, are described in Washington's words in Margaret Brown Klapthor and Howard Alexander Morrison, *G. Washington: A Figure upon the Stage* (Washington, DC: Smithsonian Institution Press, 1982). This exhibition catalog is also the source for data on Washington's false teeth, first of ivory, then of wood.

Of the many press descriptions of the farewell at Fraunces Tavern, most appear to be derived from the *Pennsylvania Packet*. Benjamin Tallmadge's recollections of the reoccupation of New York and the Fraunces Tavern farewell—much the most detailed account of the farewell—are in his *Memoir of Colonel Benjamin Tallmadge* (New York: New York Times, 1968; repr. from the 1858 edition in *Eyewitness Accounts of the American Revolution*).

The defection from the *Assistance* is reported in the *Massa-*

chusetts Sun and Worcester Gazette, January 22, 1784, under a January 7, 1784 dateline from New York, in the same edition as it carried the report from Annapolis of Washington's final farewell. Franklin's wry description of the bald eagle (on the Cincinnati emblem) as "a bird of bad moral character" is in a letter to his daughter quoted in Callahan's *Henry Knox*. His accepting honorary membership is in Garry Wills, *Cincinnatus: George Washington and the Enlightenment* (New York: Doubleday, 1984). Judge Burke's pamphlet prophesying that the Society of the Cincinnati foreshadowed tyranny appeared in the *South Carolina Gazette* in the issues of May 13–15, 1784.

7
TO PHILADELPHIA

"New Jersey is our country!" is from Catherine Drinker Bowen's *Miracle at Philadelphia* (see chap. 1, above). Elias Boudinot's letter to GW, written on January 11, 1784, is printed in full in Barbara Louise Clark's *E.B. The Story of Elias Boudinot IV: His Family, His Friends, and His Country* (Philadelphia: Dorrance and Co., 1977). Humphreys' recollections of the journey through New Jersey are from his biography of GW and its editorial notes. Texts of addresses to GW and his responses, as well as the identities of the aides who wrote them, are in the GW *Papers*. Details of the journey are from the Philadelphia press; the anonymous verses on peace are by Philip Freneau. The order by the trustees of the College of New Jersey to replace the cannonball-destroyed portrait of George II with one of Washington is an editorial note in the Peale memoirs (see notes to chap. 8).

The *Pennsylvania Packet* printed most of the addresses presented to GW in Philadelphia, as well as his responses. The City Tavern and other contemporary buildings and streets are described in Richard Webster, *Philadelphia Preserved: Catalog of the Historic American Buildings Survey* (Philadelphia: Temple University Press, 1976). Postwar Philadelphia society, including the Dancing Assembly, is detailed in Horace Mather Lippincott, *Early Philadelphia: Its People, Life and Progress* (Philadelphia: Lippincott, 1917) and in Robert C. Alberts, *The Golden Voyage* (see chap. 3). The state of restored commerce in the city is described from the *Pennsylvania Gazette* in issues of December 1783. Israel Trask's service reminiscence of Washington with Billy Lee is in John C. Dann, *The Revolution Remembered: Eyewitness Accounts of the War for Independence* (Chicago: University of Chicago Press, 1980).

David Rittenhouse's grinding of Washington's lenses and repairs to his theodolite are described in Brooke Hindle's David Rittenhouse (Princeton: Princeton University Press, 1964). Rittenhouse's observations on the transit of Venus, he notes, were made from his farm at Norriton, north of Philadelphia, rather than in the State House Yard as often described.

Peter Jay's registering his dislike of a ministerial prayer for King George is noted in a letter to him, December 12, 1783, from Governor William Livingston of New Jersey, a family friend, in Robert Morris, ed., *John Jay. The Winning of the Peace*.

Morris's cajoling of Quaker worthies for funds is described by G. W. P. Custis in his *Recollections* (see chap. 4). John Paul Jones's plea to Morris is quoted from a letter he wrote in Philadelphia on October 13, 1783, in Elizabeth M. Nuxoll and Mary A. Gallagher eds., *The Papers of William Morris*, vol. 8 (Pittsburgh: University of Pittsburgh Press, 1995). Much other documentation on Morris is from this volume. However much Morris enriched himself in commerce, the aspersions by Merrill

Jensen in *The New Nation* (above), that Morris's "disinterested patriotism" was a "myth" and that he did not "take office" to finance the war "until the Revolution was virtually over" are not sustained by the facts. He became by title Superintendent of Finances only in 1781 but had been the major financier of the Revolution under other titles since 1776.

Major John Armstrong, Jr.'s grim comments about the state of the disintegrating army appear in a letter to General Horatio Gates, May 9, 1783, quoted by Merrill Jensen in *The New Nation* (above).

8
ARTS AND ENTERTAINMENTS

That GW's expense accounts *"all in his own hand writing"* were widely public knowledge is manifest not only from the *Pennsylvania Gazette* but from the account in the *American Herald & General Advertiser*, Boston, February 9, 1784. Benjamin West's admiration of GW and his conversation about him with George III are recounted by Robert C. Alberts in *Benjamin West: A Biography* (Boston: Houghton Mifflin, 1978).

For Patience Wright and her artist son Joseph Wright and their relations with Washington see Charles Coleman Sellers, *Patience Wright. American Artist and Spy in George III's London* (Middletown, CT: Wesleyan University Press, 1976, chapters XIII and XIV.

Charles Willson Peale's relations with GW, including portrait sittings and the erection of the ill-fated triumphal arch, are described by Robert Plate in *Charles Willson Peale: Son of Liberty, Father of Art and Science* (New York: McKay, 1967) and by Charles Coleman Sellers in *Charles Willson Peale* (New York:

Scribner's, 1969, a revision of his 1947 biography which was vol. 23, parts 1 and 2, of the Memoirs of the American Philosophical Society.) Sellers reproduces an early re-creation of the design. GW's confession that his ego was massaged by posing for portraits is in a letter to Hopkinson, May 16, 1785, in Hastings, *Life and Works of Francis Hopkinson* (above).

Jacob Hiltzheimer's description of GW's departure from Philadelphia is from *Extracts from the Diary of Jacob Hiltzheimer of Philadelphia: 1765–1798* (Philadelphia: Wm. F. Fell & Co., 1893).

9
TOWARD ANNAPOLIS

Elias Boudinot (see Clark's *E.B.*, above) wrote to Benjamin Franklin on November 1, 1783 to remind him that future treaty language had to employ the new language to describe the state of Delaware. It was Boudinot's last day as President of Congress. GW's tipping express riders and other last days' expenses are on the final page of his manuscript account book, HM 5502, Huntington Library. William Ellery's letter of December 19, to Benjamin Huntington of Connecticut, is in *Letters of Delegates to Congress*. John Dickinson's message to Pennsylvania delegates in Congress about a pension for GW and their response is in *Pennsylvania Archives: Selected and Arranged from Original Documents, Commencing 1783*, vol. X (Philadelphia: Joseph Severn and Co., 1854). Accounts of GW's receptions in Wilmington, Baltimore, and Annapolis, largely overlapping, appear in press accounts from Philadelphia (as in the *Pennsylvania Gazette*, covering Wilmington) northward to the *American Herald and General Advertiser* of Boston and the *New-Hampshire Gazette* of Portsmouth.

Moore's "A Visit from St. Nicholas" and its apparent debt to

"Old Santeclaus" in *The Children's Friend* are in Stephen Nissenbaum, *The Battle for Christmas* (New York: Knopf, 1996), which reprints "Old Santeclaus." For the Puritan condemnation of Christmas in New England, see Penne L. Restad, *Christmas in America: A History* (New York: Oxford University Press, 1995). How the Old South used the Yule log is described in Julian Boyd, *Christmas at Monticello* (New York: Oxford University Press, 1964) and William Sansom, *A Book of Christmas* (New York, McGraw-Hill, 1968). Elizabeth Drinker's description of Quaker Philadelphia at Christmas is in Sarah Blank Dine ed., *The Diary of Elizabeth Drinker* (Boston: Northeastern University Press, 1991). GW's Christmas instructions to his gardener, Philip Bater, are quoted in John C. Fitzpatrick, *George Washington Himself: A Common-Sense Biography Written from His Manuscripts* (Indianapolis, Bobbs-Merrill, 1933).

The address to GW in Baltimore, and his response, are in J. Thomas Scharf, *The Chronicles of Baltimore, Being a Complete History of "Baltimore Town" and Baltimore City* (Baltimore, Turnbull Brothers, 1874).

10
FINAL FAREWELLS

Elias Boudinot's apology to Mynheer van Berckel is quoted by many sources; here it is taken from Edmond Cody Burnett, *The Continental Congress* (New York: Norton, 1964). Accounts of GW in Annapolis largely cite the same sources, primarily press accounts, such as in the *Pennsylvania Gazette*, James McHenry's letter, December 23, 1783, to Margaret Caldwell, and James Tilton's to Gunning Bedford, Jr., December 25, 1783, both in *Letters of Delegates to Congress*. Other correspondence in *Letters to Delegates* is also extracted in this chapter: Jefferson's to Gerry and McHenry, December 21, 1783, on lines in the address prepared for Mifflin that would later be excised; McHenry's earlier letter to Miss Caldwell, also December 21; David Howell's letter, December 24, 1783 to William Greene; and Abiel Foster's to Meshech Weare, December 26, 1783. Howell's deploring (to Jonathan Arnold) Annapolis's pleasures is also in *Letters to Delegates*.

George Mann's bill and particulars for catering the final banquet and ball for Washington are found (in pounds) in Paul Wilstach, *Tidewater Maryland* (Indianapolis: Bobbs-Merrill, 1931) and in dollars in Charles Thomson's memorandum book (as Secretary of Congress) for April 1784 in *Letters of Delegates to Congress*.

The tongue-in-cheek "LOST" advertisement is quoted from a London newspaper in the *Boston Gazette*, December 22, 1783. Thomas Jefferson's role in the resignation ceremony is documented in Julian P. Boyd et al., *The Papers of Thomas Jefferson*, vol. 6 (see above). Included as appendices are the Reports of the Committee on Arrangements for the audience, Jefferson's memo to McHenry and Gerry on his draft, and the committee-written response of Thomas Mifflin, each annotated to identify changes in the drafts. Also in Boyd is TJ's letter on Christmas Eve to Governor Harrison.

Madison's comment that the resignation was "a glorious action" is quoted from his post-presidential conversation with Trumbull in Stuart Leibeger *Founding Friendship: George Washington, James Madison and the Creation of the American Republic* (Charlottesville: University of Virginia Press, 2002). For Jefferson's astronomical letter on Buffon and Hopkinson's response and "Christmas Gambol," see *The Papers of Thomas Jefferson*, vol. 6 (above). John Marshall's letter to James Monroe appears in *The Papers of John Marshall*, vol. 1, Herbert A. Johnson et al., eds. (Chapel Hill: University of North Carolina Press, 1974).

11
CHRISTMAS AND AFTER

The description of Washington's uniform and sword as hung in his wardrobe on Christmas Eve is from Benson J. Lossing, *The Home of Washington, or Mount Vernon and Its Associations, Historical, Biographical and Pictorial* (Hartford: A. S. Hale, 1870), which includes Lossing's engravings of the General's clothes and sword then on display in the Patent Office in the Capital. GW's letter to Jonathan Trumbull is in the *Papers, Confederation Series,* vol. 1 (Charlottesville: University Press of Virginia, 1992). Martha Washington's letter, possibly written in October 1789 but undated, is in Mercy Otis Warren's *History of the Rise, Progress and Termination of the American Revolution* (Boston: Manning and Loring, 1805) in the reprint edition edited by Lester H. Cohen (Indianapolis: Liberty Fund, 1988).

The reference to "Christmas Pyes" in a letter to Humphreys, December 26, 1786, is from the Washington *Papers.* Although Mount Vernon was " . . . locked in snow and ice since Christmas" (Washington *Papers*), an undated letter from an unidentified "young girl from Fredericksburg" quoted in Helen Bryan's *Martha Washington: First Lady of Liberty* (New York: John Wiley, 2002) claims otherwise and also alleges that Martha had "come home on Christmas Eve" with her husband, presumably from Annapolis. "I must tell you," she writes (to "a friend"), "what a charming day I spent at Mount Vernon with Mama and Sally. The General and Madame came home on Christmas Eve, and such a racket the servants made, for they were glad of their coming. Three handsome young officers came with them. All Christmas afternoon people came to pay their Respects and Duty. Among them were stately Dames and gay young Women. The Gen'l seemed very happy and Mistress Washington was from Daybreak making everything as agreeable as possible for Everybody."

The bubbly letter has the ring of reality, but if Christmas weather was as Washington wrote to Trumbull and to Lafayette, and Mifflin to Washington, the house did not fill up with guests, nor does the General write to anyone of entertaining a houseful of company. (To Lafayette he recalled on February 1, 1784, "On the eve of Christmas I entered these doors an older man by near nine years, than when I left them. Since that period, we have been fast locked up in frost and snow, and excluded in a manner from all kinds of intercourse.") Nor did the General bring home with him three handsome young officers: there were literally only two, and one of these was the quite unhandsome David Humphreys. No other apparently authentic document places Martha anywhere but at Mount Vernon during the noontime resignation ceremony at Annapolis on December 23, and that "Mistress" Washington (generally referred to as "Lady Washington") was up as hostess "from daybreak" seems equally unlikely. The letter, its source not furnished, seems unreliable in all aspects. Stuart Leiberger in *Founding Friendships* (see above) notes that Madison helped Trumbull choose four episodes to commemorate the Revolution and that Trumbull in the resignation canvas "took the license of inserting Madison (and Martha Washington) in the picture, which now hangs in the United States Capitol."

Mifflin's letter to Washington on December 28, 1783 and Edward Hand's letter to Jasper Yeates, December 30, 1783, are both in *Letters of Delegates*. GW's query to Thomson is in the *Washington Letters*. The commission not returned to GW is in the Library of Congress.

ACKNOWLEDGMENTS

For assistance in making this book possible I offer here my appreciation to Erica W. Austin, Barbara E. Benson, Randall Blackwell, William Duncan, Robert C. Doyle, David Essmiller, Douglas Greenfield, Steven Greenfield, Frank E. Grizzard, Jr., Gary Lustig, Rena Mincks, Bruce Nichols, Francis O'Neill, William A. Pencak, Susan Reighard, Casey Reivich, John Rhodehamel, Barbara Ryan, Ira Simon, Iris Snyder, Andrea Weber, David Weintraub, Herbert Weintraub, Rodelle Weintraub, Walter Wells, Donna Williams, Richard E. Winslow III, and Peter Zimmerman.

I am also grateful to the Maryland Historical Society, the New York Historical Society, the Pennsylvania Historical Society, the Huntington Library, and the Papers of George Washington (University of Virginia).

INDEX

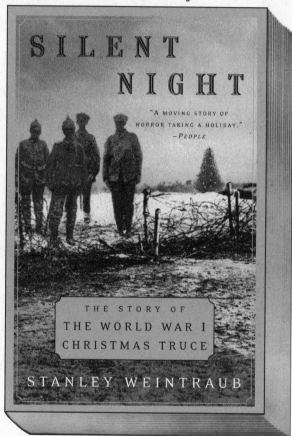